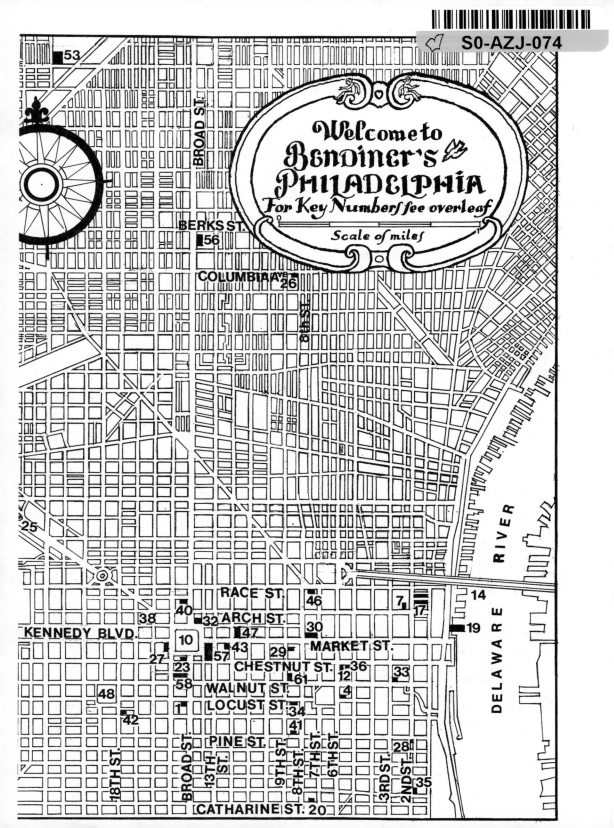

Welcome to
Bendiner's
PHILADELPHIA
For Key Numbers see overleaf
Scale of miles

WELCOME TO BENDINER'S PHILADELPHIA

Bendiner's Philadelphia

Bendiner's

Preface by Robert Bendiner

FRANKLIN PUBLISHING COMPANY

BY ALFRED BENDINER

PHILADELPHIA

Library of Congress Catalogue Card Number: 76-3105
ISBN   0-87133-0695

First Printing, November 1964
Second Printing, December 1964
Third Printing, April 1966
Paperback Edition
First Printing, April 1976

These drawings and texts with some modifications appeared originally
in the Sunday Philadelphia **Bulletin** Magazine
and are here reprinted by permission.

Also by *Alfred Bendiner*

MUSIC TO MY EYES
TRANSLATED FROM THE HUNGARIAN

Printed in the United States of America

PREFACE

In my occasional visits to the City of Brotherly Love over the years, I became more familiar with Philadelphia's Bendiners than with Bendiner's Philadelphia. That should disqualify me, perhaps, to write a preface for a book on that city's architecture, and if the book were by anyone but my cousin Alfred, the disqualification would stand. But since the volume tells as much about its author as it does about buildings or bridges or parks, I feel as warranted in doing the job as the next fellow—as long as the next fellow is not, as he was, a Fellow of the American Institute of Architects.

At some time in the course of his training, Al committed to memory, probably under compulsion, a classic passage on what is needed to make an architect, to wit: "He must be an artist or his buildings will offend the eye, an engineer or they will crumble, a lawyer or he will get us all into trouble, a doctor or they will be hygienically unfit to live in, a businessman and a contractor and, last but not least, he must be a gentleman or we will have nothing to do with him."

While my cousin claimed to believe that this multiple injunction "put the stuffy curse" on his profession, he actually thought these requirements insufficient; so he added the professions of caricaturist, writer, archaeologist, raconteur and wit. Somehow he skipped politician and he generally gave diplomacy a wide berth, but practically every other interest of man was a personal interest of his—from baseball, which he loved in spite of having had to put up with the Phillies in their worst years, to the newspaper business, which he fondly believed to have been better before it abandoned its Front Page rattiness for the comforts of sanitized surroundings.

What the layman should easily discover in these pages is precisely this combination of breadth of interest and irreverence of spirit. The first was a measure of the man's genial affection for all things human. The second was an indication of his effort to keep that affection decently under wraps, perhaps out of a wholesome fear of being thought sentimental. In truth he was not sentimental at all; he was uncommonly and refreshingly honest. But he was good-humored, too; and, being good-humored, he saw the fun in the world that offsets, at least some of the time, its miseries.

He saw enough fun in Philadelphia, at any rate, to make these pages at once glorify the city and endear it to other Americans in this bicentennial year—not as a museum piece to be studied in awe, but as a living community that has colorfully evolved since the days when Franklin viewed it with a similarly shrewd and lively eye. It is easy to imagine Old Ben's shade enjoying this book, perhaps even wishing he had been given a chance to print it—as a public service, a sound investment and, not least, a labor of love.

ROBERT BENDINER, 1976
Huntington, N.Y.

Acknowledgements

Our thanks to John Harbeson, distinguished architect, educator and writer, for creating the map which welcomes you to Bendiner's Philadelphia in this new edition. Dr. Harbeson is internationally known. He and Al Bendiner were friends for many years.

Additional thanks to Robert Bendiner for contributing the preface. He is the author of "Just Around The Corner, a Highly Selective History of the Thirties," among other works, and is a member of the Editorial Board of The New York Times.

Bendiner's Philadelphia was initially Bernard Bergman's idea, and no edition should be printed without grateful acknowledgement. Mr. Bergman is Book Editor of The Evening and Sunday Bulletin.

CONTENTS

Bendiner's Philadelphia

GERMANTOWN HOUSE

(Requiescat in pace)

In those awful days not so long ago, before Philadelphia was corrupt and discontented, there used to be a lot of people around here who enjoyed gracious living, peace and calm, quiet contentment in a house just like this one.

I forget where it is but it doesn't matter any more. It's probably torn down for a filling station, an apartment house or it blocked a superhighway.

This kind of home was of stone, with walls thick enough to brag about, and in the stair newel post there was set a circular white ivory piece to show that the whole house had been paid for. Inside there was plenty of room to swing a cat and have four or five kids.

The place was always drafty in the winter. In summer it didn't matter because at the first sign of heat the family went to Cape May or Bar Harbor and the house was solidly boarded up, the furniture completely enveloped in white linen covers, the rugs camphored and rolled, straw matting covered the floors and the gas light fixture was entombed in gauze.

Around the outside perimeter of the first floor ran a wood porch wide enough for a swing, and there were wicker settees, rockers and tables covered with white linen embroidery.

The house was usually perched high on a hill so that it was hard to get the carriage up to the front steps and in winter there was a lot of snow shoveling to be done. In the summer the porch decoration was milk bottles and a week's supply of *The Evening Bulletin*, until Pop remembered to stop it.

About the house were tall trees and on the lawns a stray iron stag. The floral display was those awful hydrangeas or R.R. station flowers.

But that was before the Democrats and goodness and two cars in every quarter acre.

1

THE ACADEMY OF
THE FINE ARTS

Frank Furness, Architect, 1871

Now that the architectural historians cry into their sleeve handkerchiefs every time somebody dares to touch a single stone of Frank Furness' architecture, I guess we'll have the building of The Pennsylvania Academy of the Fine Arts with us for some time.

It is one of the greatest conglomerations of artistic hand-me-downs ever put together into a building and it maintains a consistency inside and outside of foliated nothing in brick, marble and cast iron.

But there it is, and try and modernize it. Joe Fraser, the director, does a heroic job trying to screen a piece here and light a room there, and make believe that Benjamin West's "Death on a Pale Horse" looks good alongside a Jackson Pollock dripping.

Furness was the only architect who earned the Medal of Honor on the field of battle in the Civil War. Then he plastered Philadelphia with his architecture and let Louis Sullivan work in his office. He looked out the window at the Jayne Building, which inspired him, and hence Frank Lloyd Wright, and on down to the architecture we have today.

This is a nice short history of modern architecture and who started it all: Frank Furness.

If you like The Pennsylvania Academy of The Fine Arts building you would have just loved the Broad St. Station, the B and O Station, the Library of the University of Pennsylvania and the Rodef Shalom Synagogue, some churches, houses, banks and a lot of other buildings.

But they all stood in the way of Progress, so you don't have to worry any more. Just go and look at that Furness period piece, the P.A. of the F.A., and see what you missed.

3

UNION LEAGUE

And then there is that one about the visitor and the Philadelphian walking down South Broad street.

"What is that building?" asked the visitor.

"That," said the Philadelphian, "is the Union League."

"What's the crepe on the door for?" asked the visitor.

"I guess one of the members died," answered the Philadelphian.

"Cheers it up some, doesn't it?" remarked the visitor.

The Union League is where all good Republicans go to die. I think they now recognize Roosevelt, if you voted only once. The late Jack Kelly, Democrat, once walked up the front steps, blueing up a lot of tired blood and driving the old seat-holders to an extra hot milk and bourbon.

If you can get a foot inside the door, it is still Victorian Saratoga hotel or Mississippi riverboat, beautiful, and the food is much too good for the common people.

CITY HALL

City Hall is as Philadelphia as the water and Sunday. It follows the laws of architecture in that it is useful as well as beautiful. Every new administration blats about tearing it down and then spends a lot of tax money fixing it up.

It is an ornate European swoon with lots of statuary by the late Alexander Milne Calder whose well-remembered son did the Logan Square fountain and whose grandson does mobiles.

If you look at the place through bird-watcher glasses you can see the beautiful bird-coated sculpture, stone lucarnes, foliates and floriates.

Inside is a fine, spacious courthouse and government home. The rooms are lofty and ornate. The offices are large enough so that any councilman or judge can walk up and down, and his walls can just about handle a four-year collection of framed photographs showing "himself" shaking hands with dignitaries, plaque bearers, Miss Philadelphias, his mama and pop and all the family.

Then there are the testimonial plaques, gavels, loving cups, Democratic donkeys and gracious gifts of ship models, cigar boxes and other impedimenta from prisoner 22564321— the one he let off with only 20 years.

The courtyard used to be swell when the Black Marias and paddy wagons pulled up from Moyamensing and delivered the desperate characters into the maw of the prisoner's tower.

There were a couple of characters in the hall once. Like Ikey Pinwheel, whose ears wiggled, and Chippy Patterson, in his crummy bulletholed cap, and that mysterious MO, Nick Hayes.

But that was long ago and far away under those naughty Republicans. Now it's all clean and even the starlings are chased away. . . .

FIRST CITY TROOP

First Troop City Cavalry is a distinguished dragoon organization of the steel-rimmed glasses set. They turn out resplendent and mounted if they can get the horses, when royalty or Republicans visit, or also on Thanksgiving Day to go to church, unmounted.

But in war times, they fight valiantly just as a good soldier should.

Generally the troop is composed of gentlemen whose pictures in uniform only appear in swish photographers' windows, except maybe Dr. J. William White. He was a noted doctor and a sort of amateur roughneck who was surgeon to the troop.

Once he appeared at a dinner in full troop regalia. Some brash trooper whose identity is shrouded in mystery told Dr. White he was not properly dressed because as surgeon he was not entitled to wear the uniform.

I guess Dr. White took off his brand new buckskin gauntlet and slapped his informant across the face and challenged him to a duel. This was the last duel in Philadelphia and was held in Rittenhouse Square in full view of the early morning resters in the windows of the Rittenhouse Club on May 18, 1880, new style, I think. Both duellers fired and both missed.

Legend has it that Dr. White walked over,

shook hands with his opponent and said, "I fired into the air."

His adversary said, "I didn't, I fired right at you."

"To that fact," said Dr. White, "I owe my life."

The armory and drill floor are still standing at 23rd and Ranstead Streets, and the building is the crenellated rustication so dear to the hearts of the old French military architects Vauban and Viollet le Duc and their followers and little boys who still have romantic notions about soldiers.

Except that nowadays the place is loaded with jeeps, half-tracks, tanks and artillery and smells gasoline and oil instead of the nice brown, damp, earthy lovely smell of stables and horses and leather.

So nowadays troopers have to ride scrounged Park Guard horses and livery stable oat burners and whatever Main Line hackers are around.

For now the First City Troop is officially known as Troop A, First Reconnaissance Squadron, 103d Armor, of Pennsylvania's 28th National Guard Division.

Ah me, things just aren't the same.

8

UNDER THE EAGLE

Nearly everybody in Philadelphia who reads The Bulletin sits at some time under the tail feathers of the John Wanamaker store eagle, waiting and looking at his watch. It's a custom, like throwing a coin into the fountain of the Trevi, only cheaper.

John Wanamaker bought the eagle from the Japanese Exhibit at the Louisiana Purchase Exhibition in St. Louis in 1904 and had it polished. It is the American eagle, made in Frankfurt, Germany, for the Japanese government and everything about it is very eagle and delicately modeled and cast and polished with every feather neatly in place. It fell through the floor once but now it is secure.

Usually you have enough time to examine every last detail while waiting for your wife to show up.

Around and about swirls the great white marble court, which is never left alone to enjoy like a big old candy box or a Barocco Roccoco Renaissance theatre.

No, no, the great organ peals mightily from its gold and white piping, or the Munkacsy paintings somber it at Easter. It is green for the Spring Festival and changes through the gay holiday spirit of Christmas. The counters, balconies and colonnades are always loaded with baubles. After all this modernism it still remains the best looking store in the country.

9

WEIGHTMAN HALL

Now that Sir Nick Skorich and his green knights have the Philadelphia Eagles flying high, the stands are again full at Franklin Field.

I would like you to pause and admire Weightman Hall or maybe I better not insist, especially when around sixty thousand raving maniacs are getting in the way, yelling and waving their hands right across the view just because Billie Barnes is cutting off tackle.

Weightman Hall is that beautiful Cambridge, England, brick red affair back of the goal posts which makes it hard to see the field goals. It is a handsome example of Collegiate Gothic Architecture so dear to the heart of misty-eyed old grads who can remember what Mike Murphy said.

It used to be a lovely background for football when the game was just for overstuffed bluebloods, "with ivy overgrown," and ready to die with their backs to the goal post, fourth down and a yard to go.

But football has moved up to professional status and the game is wide open and the goal posts have been moved back ten yards and you can't even get massacred knocking them over after the game.

But Weightman Hall still stands, lending dignity and charm to occasions which might otherwise descend to the low level of a brawl. It used to house the gymnasium and swimming pool and team dressing room and in the tower R. Tait Mackenzie, the sculptor of athletes, had his studio.

Now it's all feminine. The girls own the gym and the swimming pool and the dancing classes are in the area of the team rooms.

So hail Pennsylvania and Mike Murphy, Lawson Robertson, Billie Morris and George Kistler and all the others.

PENN CENTER

It's a shame about Penn Center. It just seems like yesterday that the Pennsylvania Railroad ran its tracks right into the heart of the city, coming to a crummy stop at the Broad Street Station, an architectural horror attached to a fine copy of a London terminal.

The railroad had decided to tear it down and did so just as the Democrats came in. This left a clear band of real estate about a quarter-mile wide, free and clear for the development of the city. The itchy, arty fingers of the planners proceeded with fancy models and layouts to show the owners how to do it. But nobody around here bit, so New York operators were brought in to develop it. The result is a series of uninspired, already outdated mediocrity.

The dream that was supposed to rival the Piazza San Marco in Venice or Rockefeller Center in New York hardly holds a candle to anything worth remembering or photographing. Now the undertakers of architecture, the landscape boys, have dropped plants and dwarf trees around and filled the "bear pits"

to the railroad concourse with plaster sculpture.

I guess it's a good example of how fast the gobbledygook planners change their theories. The first two buildings have a solid, glary, glassy stare, very popular about 25 years ago.

Then there's the Transportation Building with a mile of unrelieved ribbons of alternating stone and windows, very popular modern theory about 20 years ago. Then a new hotel with aluminum spandrels, very popular about 15 years ago. And now off in left field a circular glass box marked "Hospitality Center," very popular in der Bauhaus 35 years ago.

So you see if we keep going forward backwards we will probably get some nice human-scale Georgian, very popular a couple of hundred years ago, after they tear down City Hall. Then in Penn Center we can have a whole history of Modern Architecture without a single distinguished example.

Of course there is always the PSFS Building which nobody has come even close to in 30 years.

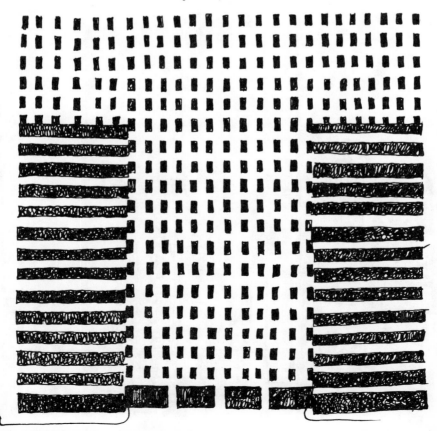

HARRISON BUILDING

Probably the most often passed-without-ever-looking-at building in central Philadelphia is the Harrison Building at 15th and Market Streets, southwest corner.

If you went to France and had someone translate through the garlic what the American Express French guide was saying, you would realize suddenly that here is an inspiration from the Francois Premier style, by the great Philadelphia architects Walter Cope and John Stewardson.

It is a well-studied, elaborately detailed chateau type, so dear to the heart of visitors to the Loire.

Of course, the first floor line is "improved Philadelphia"—a maze of interesting bargain hardware stores, pizzerias, bookezines, pawn shops and animal pet shops which every normal bargain lover and marketer thinks ought to be allowed to exist on a street appropriately named Market Street.

But no, no, every once in so often the old crocks of the art jury get chattering about pulling down the signs and artying the place up. They're even talking about tearing it down and putting up a brand new building—to match, I suppose, those great gems across the street in Penn Center.

14

THE ARENA

Boxing was a fine art when I was a boy and also you had to know some means of self-defense because psychiatrists hadn't been invented for juveniles. I learned the hard way and also at Billy Herrmann's gymnasium, where Marine Captain Anthony J. Drexel Biddle, Jr., the blue-blood amateur prize-fighter hung out, and he gave me a cup for proficiency.

But my teacher was Young Jack O'Brien, who was the kid brother of Gentleman Jack O'Brien, the light heavyweight champion of the whole world. You were supposed to stand in the center of the ring and pivot while Young Jack O'Brien danced around and boxed you and gave you a paste in the snoot every once in a while. Young Jack had a glass jaw and many times boxers reached it, but not me.

Like a lot of things now past, Philadelphia used to be a good boxing town with small clubs like the Cambria Athletic Club run by Johnny Burns of the Iron Hat, The Nonpareil, Olympic and National. Now things are bigger and so the Arena has for years served as a local Madison Square Garden. Within its purely functional barn-like interior many boxers and just plain fighters have danced in the glare of the ring lights and were introduced by a hog caller affectionately known as "Babe" O'Rourke.

To be a real boxing buff you should remember the Dempsey-Tunney long count at the Stadium, or Benny Leonard getting his hair mussed by Lew Tendler, or Tommy Loughran being serenaded by St. Monica's Boys Band, or Mat Adgie, Jimmy Fryer, Joe Brown, Willie Clarke, Harry Blitman, Pete Nebo, Tony Canzoneri, and other worthies.

The most interesting moment in boxing at the Arena, for me, was the night Benny Bass fought a return match with Chesty Joe Firpo from Pennsgrove, New Jersey, who in the first fight made the big mistake of knocking about Mr. Benny Bass. The place was loud with New Jersey, and Chesty Joe Firpo's followers had brought along a band and a big horse-shoe of roses which they draped around his waiting tense form. The ring bell sounded and without any of the usual glove-shaking formalities Benny Bass walked across the ring and just as Firpo was slowly rising from his stool Mr. Bass clipped him one on the button and Chesty Joe Firpo fell back into his bouquet of roses and lay there.

The great boxing brag around Philadelphia was Dr. J. William White, the famous society surgeon who put up his dukes endlessly and without much provocation.

Legend has it that he was once seated in the audience in a New York arena when the announcer announced with a sneer that the next bout was forfeited because the fighter from Philadelphia hadn't shown up. Dr. White arose and climbed into the ring, took off his Prince Albert coat but not his white vest, took off his starched cuffs and adjusted the boxing gloves, walked to the center of the ring and with a single blow knocked cold the New Yorker, thereby upholding the honor and name of Philadelphia.

15

THE BARNES
FOUNDATION

Designed by a Frenchman, Paul Phillipe Cret, to house a fine collection of Frenchmen's paintings—Renoir, Manet, Monet, Jacquet, acquired by a bush league second baseman rough guy who took great pleasure in keeping most people from seeing his lovelies, except maybe his private collection of students.

A tragic death and then taxes have finally, with the aid of a hot blast of Judge Anne X. Alpern, the state's erstwhile attorney general, opened up the vault to public gaze. I mean two hundred weekly.

Well, here you are in the Jeu de Paume except only surrounded by highly polished Pennsylvania farmhouse hardware. But go, by all means. A little easier to get to than Paris, but when you come out, where are you? Merion, Pa.

16

THE CIRCUS

About fifty years ago when I was an art department copy boy on the Ledgers I fell in love with Lillian Leitzel who was doing the giant half flange of 240 overarms on the solo rope with the Barnum & Bailey circus at 19th and Hunting Park. Miss Leitzel was only about ten years my senior and was then in love with Alfred Codona, who was trying to win her by doing the triple forward somersault from the high trapeze.

I lost Miss Leitzel but gained a great love for the circus and everybody who could ride an elephant or do a tinsiker. In my cover painting for this illustrious publication (a little apple polishing won't hurt), is everybody who was in the rings on a cold Sunday afternoon last March in Madison Square Garden. I came home with a high fever, a throat full of elephant dust and an upset stomach from too many hot dogs, lemonade, pink candy floss and two bags of peanuts.

For weeks at night Emmett Kelly, Lou Jacobs, 16 midgets in a kid's fire engine and a troupe of elephants climbed over me while acrobats did triple somersaults, beautiful babes rocked in the trunks of smelly elephants, lions roared and bears rolled over.

Only it wasn't nearly as good as when I was a boy and Fred Bradna was ringmaster and Merle Evans led the band and of course Roland Butler was the advance man with the familiar press agent's spiel of "The supreme spectacle symbolizing in extravaganza, amusing fantasy and processional splendor the heart root forms which have inspired humanity with costumes of imaginative prodigality and 20,000 people and animals enacting humorous and nostalgic roles which will be long remembered."

STRAWBERRY MANSION
BRIDGE

The Strawberry Bridge—I guess you could call it that—doesn't seem right for automobile traffic because it was designed to carry the horse-and-buggy set and mainly the park trolley, so dear to the heart of geriatrics.

The park trolleys used to run through the woodlands and the dell lands of Fairmount Park and served fresh, cool air on hot summer nights to poor and tired families at a nickel a head.

If you swung on early you could grab the outside seat right back of the motorman and hang out over the guard chain and really get a blast of fresh air. But we were never allowed to sit in the last three rows because they were reserved for smokers.

When you grew tall enough to hang on, no growing boy would consider it manly just to sit. He could stand on the step which ran the length of the open cars and hold on to the rail and jump on and off when the car was in motion. But riding out of the woods and down the slope to the bridge was real sport because you could hang out over the edge and spit 'way down, perhaps hitting a sculler if you were real lucky.

I guess the bridge is very special and so high and wide and the biggest span in the world for 1870, but who cares except the commissioner of Fairmount Park and bridge engineers?

And anyhow, kids nowadays would think it corny to ride the car step and wing out when they can drag-race and break their necks more easily, or at least be annoying to their elders in other ways.

19

THE MERCHANTS
EXCHANGE

Formerly the Stock Exchange and later the Merchants Exchange and later nothing much but a lovely, ratty market where you went for Christmas trees and wreaths.

It is now being restored to its original glory and is filled with government do-gooders of the National Park Service.

Designed by Strickland in 1834, it is in the gracious classic spirit, with a bowed Greek Corinthian colonnade and capped by an over-sized copy of the Choragic monument of Lysycraties. Pardon me while I get my "Classic Antiquities" out of the upper shelf.

It stands at Walnut and 3d in the midst of devastation which your children may enjoy as rebuilt Society Hill.

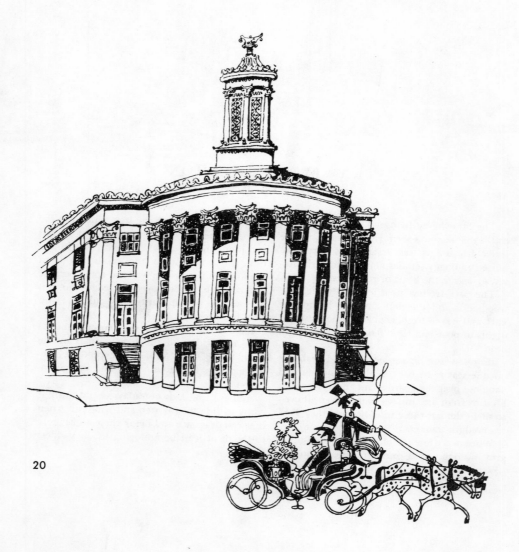

20

FAIRMOUNT PARK
FOUNTAIN

Of all things, Moses, screaming at the children of Israel from Mount Sinai, now playing as the central theme of the Catholic Total Abstinence Union Fountain, at the 52nd Street entrance of Fairmount Park.

Standing on four individual park water fountains with their backs to Moses and his old Ten Commandments, and apparently not listening to one word, are Bishop Carroll, Father Matthew, Charles Carroll, and Commodore Barry.

The fountain was dedicated in 1876, and when I was a boy, YOUKNOWHO knocked poor old Moses's head off with a well-placed bolt of lightning, but the Catholic Total Abstinence Union cemented it right back on again.

GUARDHOUSE IN
THE PARK

This little gem of Victorian jigsaw scroll-work wood architecture, over by the Museum of Art, has been a guardhouse since about 1850. Along with the romantic garden pavilion up on Fairmount it stands as a sweet, wisteria sentiment to the dear, dead Victorian Gothic days.

Happily, these delightful wood creations by an unknown hand are under the jurisdiction of the Fairmount Park Commission, which is a lot more tolerant of fine olde things than the shillelagh and pole-ax wielders down in City Hall.

How or why it has been spared the ax as unworthy, is something I wish I hadn't brought up. I guess it is full of termites and not much use as a guardhouse but it should serve as some kind of a reminder that carpentry was a fine art and something to be sighed for, now that we always have reinforced concrete shoved down our throats as beautiful, beautiful.

The style is pointed Gothic or maybe perpendicular or maybe most people don't even know Gothic. There used to be lots of these guardhouses along the Drive.

As I remember, it mainly used to house a poor, tired, fat park guard who waved to you as you rode home from funerals in the black hacks. He was encouraged by a big cigar which my father always gave cops—just to be on the safe side.

Anyhow, there it still stands and it was there long before the Parkway and the Museum and Herr Dr. Siemering's bronze statue of Frederick the Grosser now passing as George Washington, riding over a zoo full of sleepy bronze animals.

And just around the corner is the wooden Acropolis now known as the Aquarium. That, too, really is wonderful woodwork, but not for long, I guess.

23

24

MY CHRISTMAS TREE

Well, finally, Merry Christmas.

What used to be a sweet and cute story-book holiday for kids now belongs to Big Business beginning at Halloween and ending when all the bills have been paid next June. Baumkuchen, candy canes, springerles and mistletoe come dully wrapped in cellophane.

But Christmas has a special sprig in memory now that Philadelphia has gone solid good and dull. In the days before this anti-payola wave you could give a cop a cigar or a schnapps or even a turkey for his kids without feeling that you were wholly immoral and corrupt.

During the boom days when everybody was rolling, we had a friend who was the vice president of an insurance company and a minister, also. The Church would hand him a couple of parishes where he could preach, sing hymns and fatten up the poor with ice cream in the summer and a big party at Christmas with turkey, magicians, and presents for the kids. We would go along at Christmas and be real pious and patronising and after the party we would all troop out to the Minister Vice President's home after dinner, help trim the tree at midnight, exchange presents and go home in the early morning light of Christmas day.

Well, this particular Christmas was a tinsel post card one with snow, ice, wind and weather. We had gone through the preliminaries and around midnight the Reverend rang for the butler and said, "And now George, bring the tree." The butler looked crestfallen and said, "Father, I didn't want to tell you, we haven't a tree. By the time I got around to getting one they were all sold out." "No tree for Christmas?" said the pastor. "That's impossible, Alfred and I will get one."

We drove through the icy night all around the Main Line but not a sprig. We drove into the City Hall area, but it too was cold, empty and desolate. Then the V.P. said, "What fools we mortals be. In my office is the biggest Christmas tree which has been serving all afternoon for the office party. Let us go and get it."

We drove to the office building. The circular door was locked. We rang and rang for the night watchman and there was no answer. We were freezing and miserable.

The Vice President Dominie said, "Let's kick the door." He kicked. There was a shower of plate glass. Bells rang. From nowhere a covey of cops started converging on us, a red car appeared.

We stood. "What goes on, boys?" said a copper. "Gentlemen," said the V.P., "I am the vice president of the insurance company on the tenth floor. I am a minister. I had no tree for Christmas and so I thought I could get the tree which decorates our office. The watchman does not answer and I kicked the door and it shattered." Then with a sweep of his arm he reached into his inside pocket and withdrew a sheaf of brand new dollar bills and sprayed them generously around the shivering bluecoats.

"Well thanks, Father, and is that all you want, a tree?" said the cops. "We'll get you a tree." We got into our car and the cops got into the red car and backed up and went sliding up the wrong way on a one-way street. A block away the caravan stopped in front of a restaurant where, flanking the entrance, were two lovely firs in wooden boxes.

"Take your choice, Father," said the officer. The Reverend looked heavenward for guidance.

"I'll take the one on the left," said he. The cops got out a couple of wire cutters and some rope. The tree was hung on the front fender like a deer and we headed homeward in the cold light of Christmas singing, "Good King Wenceslaus look'd out."

We replaced the tree the day after Christmas.

ONCE UPON
A NEW YEAR'S

Happy New Year and here's to no fallout in your eggnog.

To me, the big heroes of New Year's Days are the shivering fathers and mothers who stand in the cold for hours, with a kid perched on each shoulder or the brood balancing precariously on crates and baskets, watching the Mummers' Parade.

I was brought up with a custom which seemed a wonderful way to usher in the New Year, but I am sure it now sounds corny and cold.

My family were American citizens, immigrants from Hungary. The only time we kids were allowed to be up at midnight was New Year's Eve. I think we slept until about 11 P.M. and then we would bundle up and take the trolley to Independence Hall.

There we would stand solemnly in the cold night, with only the light in the clock face to watch. At the stroke of midnight, the bell would toll twelve times and we would wish each other a Happy New Year in the Land of the Free. Then we would go home and have a glass of wine all around and go to bed, to lie dreaming about the New Year's Shooters' parade which would be our treat for being good all year.

But New Year's Eve is a different matter now. We stand outdoors with a glass and watch the old year out, and listen to the bells and the whistles—a nice, quiet, satisfying, middle-aged way of celebrating.

28

PENN LIBRARY

When I was a little scared boy going to the Architectural School at the University of Pennsylvania a hundred years ago the first thing you were taught to thoroughly dislike was the architecture of the Library.

It was corny. It was icky. It was esthetically bad, undignified and also lacking in quality, "je ne sais quoi" and "savoir faire." It stank and was Supreme Lousy.

The other year I took Frank Lloyd Wright out to see it and he said, "It is the work of an artist."

So now that they wish to tear it down, people write letters to save it, architectural historians weep and get Ph. D.T.s at the very thought of it being demolished and I think the last word is that it is going to be made into the new Architectural School.

There are a couple of requirements of good architecture. It should be useful as well as beautiful. The library was useful to me. I met a lot of lovely coeds in the reading room when I should have been studying Vitruvius, Guadet and Vignola.

It was beautiful, once, in the cool recess of a Furness niche, when I was hiding out from a sophomore who was anxious to tear me limb from pants in the historic pants fight which then raged the campus.

So, to me, it is still Architecture and I want to reserve judgment about tearing it down until I get a chance to look around the new one.

LEARY'S BOOK STORE

Leary's Book Store on 9th Street across from the Federal Court Building maintains a certain dignity and charm and an aloofness to its surroundings.

It used to be presided over by ex-Governor Stuart's brother and he was a typical Philadelphian of the blue serge, white vest, ruddy complexion, mustache, school. Everybody else in the place was tall, thin, meerschaum-colored, wore a loose linen coat and marked the price of books in blue pencil on the hard front cover. That blue pencil mark is still the trade mark of Leary's and it is hard to erase.

There are four floors in Leary's and books are stacked from floor to ceiling and you are welcome to look at all of them as long as you want, without any salesman needling you to buy something. In addition, there is an outdoor stall which snakes across the front and down a side alley, full of even cheaper copies.

That should be enough books to satisfy anybody's craving. Most Philadelphians were weaned on Leary's second-hand ones and some new ones, starting in the basement with trots for Caesar's Gallic Wars and Xenophon's Anabasis, and all the other major irritations of school boys; then going up through novels on the first floor, rarities and travel on the second, art and medical on the third and science on the fourth. Spaced around these generalizations are all the other literary needs of man.

My father claimed that he never bought a book that cost more than ten cents and he spent a lot of spare time in Leary's proving his point and getting an education. He was an immigrant Hungarian and a fierce American citizen, so all references to Hungarians and patriotism were bought and heavily underlined in blue pencil so we kids were sure to get the full ten cents' worth.

Mr. Stuart always greeted my father by telling him that he would buy everything back, but how could you sell a book back to Leary's at this late date, especially when it is all underlined and you can't bear to erase or scratch out that fifty-year-old ten-cent mark?

The other feature of Leary's which has weathered all the art juries is the outdoor sign the height of the building above the first floor. It is of a near-sighted ancient reader standing precariously on a rickety ladder with big fat books under his arms and between his knees and held to his nose.

For years I have been trying to figure how he could turn the page without dropping one little volume, which in my training was a major crime. If we dropped a book we had to pick it up and kiss it. But that's old-school-reverence stuff and really corny nowadays.

ACADEMY OF MUSIC

One of the crummiest pigeon-coated facades in Philadelphia is that old sacred cow, The Academy of Music. Any poor lug of a businessman who wishes to put up a sign or plant a tree to make his place a little more interesting gets clobbered, but try and get rid of that Civil War farmer's market, rotting, leaky iron shed marquee and you probably will get letters to The Bulletin from Dilworth and Abe Rosen.

If you look above the tin roof, the facade is one of those architectural solutions where you spend it all on the interior and hope that the next generation will fix up the exterior brickwork and hang some marble on it.

The front entrance is composed of round head openings with glass doors. Between them are very old-fashioned glass cases holding the eight-sheet announcements which nobody but a trifocal music lover can read. They haven't changed in style since Abraham Lincoln walked through those doors to address the Republican Party.

The stage door on Locust Street is probably the most interesting entrance in Philadelphia. Through its antique portals have passed everything and everybody in music, the opera, the ballet, jazz, politics, travel and a thousand other fields which require stage presence. And also the scenery, costumes, instruments of the Orchestra men and the elephants for the second act of Aida.

The Academy is run on both sides of the footlights by two charming characters who are sorely tried by the public and the hairy geniuses.

Behind the gold bars and the "sold out" sign on the Box Office stands Mom Haly, Mrs. Catherine Haly. For thirty years she has been beaming and jovial even when she has nothing better to offer than "two in back of a column for next March." Mrs. Haly has raised children and an occasional grandchild in that Box Office with the motto "Be kind and considerate to the Public even when the Public is trying every gimmick to get two in seventh row center, or at least on the aisle."

Just to the right of the stage door and behind a gold plate sits Mr. Harold Mason, the General Manager of the building. He looks like the American's idea of a thin, worn, English schoolmaster complete with steel-rimmed glasses. And he has sucked through the stems of 384 pipes while calmly waiting for the screaming Maestros to quiet down, just because something went wrong backstage.

Of course, once you get past Mom Haly and Harold Mason you are inside the Academy and *it* gets enough publicity without my piling it on.

OLD MOKO

When Napoleon conquered Egypt he took along architects and artists to measure and draw the monuments—hence the Empire style and Moyamensing Prison by the Philadelphia architect, Thomas Ustick Walter.

Anyhow, Egyptian architecture had a vogue around these parts and the "debtors' prison" at Moyamensing is a fine exterior example of a fair copy of the temple at Edfu, only in brownstone. It has rotted to a point where it looks almost like Edfu except that there are no Egyptians around to beg for baksheesh, nor colorful donkey boys or guides in abbas and tarbooshes bragging about King Memnon. How's that for name dropping?

There are a couple of good reasons why you should hurry up and go see Moko (outside only). First, Egypt is now trying to save the well-worth-preserving beautiful temples at Abu Simbel and Philae from being inundated by the Aswan Dam across the Nile.

Moko looks something like Philae only more like Edfu, but it is here and in a poor state of preservation even for an Egyptian temple. What's more, in a couple of ·years nobody except maybe the Society of Architectural Historians is going to yap about saving it, so good-by to Thomas Ustick Walter's brownstone Egyptian front prison.

Secondly, to get to this shrine you must go to South Philadelphia, the last outpost of Democracy, where a man can own property and park his car in front of it even if he had to throw rocks at Dickie Dilworth for the privilege.

It is all perfectly safe now and quiet, if you have your passport, and also you can still buy an eel from a pushcart on the way North.

THE PICKERING HUNT

This is a hunt, and a very disorderly field at that. Unless you like hunts and hunt people you wouldn't understand, and you might affect an English accent and poke fun at a lot of earnest, hard-working people who get up early on cold and frosty mornings and help rid the countryside of that savage pest, the red fox.

I know all about being able to trap foxes or shoot them or just let them prey on your chickens so they can look lovely patterned against the fall foliage.

But fox hunting is the sport of kings, and queens and jacks and other very nice people who live on the Main Line. They are now almost reduced to drags and going up-country, what with the pushy quarter-acre and station-wagon set and their little one-horse garages and trailer vans. And also now there are no grooms except maybe some imported English girls who you really can't expect to stay unmarried and just groom horses, what with those lovely pink cheeks and strong Henry Moore figures.

If you want to see a real hunt ceremony, though, come out to the early morning annual service at the Little Church in the Great Valley near Paoli (site of the Paoli massacre). There, assembled in their dress pinks, are the masters and members and guests of the Pickering Hunt, and their mounts and a pack of hounds, quiet for a moment and attended by the whip and the honorary whip. The minister blesses the hounds and the hunt and prays for a healthy and happy and fruitful season and everybody gallops off to a late start.

After a good, healthy ride in the cold, bracing air through beautiful Chester County, there is naught as stimulating as a stirrup cup that cheers, or maybe two or three depending on how long you are waiting for the hunt to come in.

But most fun of all is lying warm and snug in a stone farmhouse and listening to the baying of the hounds and the hallooing of the whip and the crunching of the snow as the hounds, masters, whips and field go crashing along over field and stream after a flash of red fox. Some day I am determined to get right up and get strapped on a horse and gallop along. But then I couldn't see the big picture.

CITY COUNCIL

Our great Mayor has officially made up his mind to strike out on the long road to Governor, and where does that leave all of us? With the head of City Council, Mr. Tate, as Acting Mayor.

Last time I saw Mr. Tate he was running Council from his lofty eminence in The Council Chamber in City Hall. If you have never had a bill come up for final hearing or represented some foreign group or dignitary, or were trying to find a place to keep warm, it is quite likely that you have never seen where your own City is governed.

The main chamber is a large, paneled room, ornate even in Roman Emperor terms, and the king pin of all, the head of Council, sits high up on a marble throne, encrusted with gold wreaths, anthemions, swags and walls of Troy. The chair of office is a large wooden Napoleonic type of the Empire Style, as interpreted by Grand Rapids, and it is enclosed by an oversized niche flanked by Doric columns and a heavy entablature over a bolster frieze.

There is a Roman mace for declaring the meeting in session and a flanking pair of eagle-topped flags. Around and about in concentric semicircles are the heavily paneled wooden desks of the members of Council. The floor is carpeted and there is an enormous chandelier which lights up a highly carved and gilded ceiling.

Of course the most incongruous addition to all this opulence and elegance are the members of Council, who should be dressed in Roman togas and speak florid Shakespearean Julius Caesar English. But mostly they look like you and even me and their grammar and diction are not always above reproach.

With all the complications attending the departure of a Mayor who I thought was dedicated to Philadelphia but now seems bent on being Governor of Pennsylvania, it brings up a lot of Charter mumbo jumbo which will take time to explain.

Anyhow, at least you now know what the hot seat looks like and whoever sits in it will probably be able and capable of taking the brickbats and bouquets which are the natural heritage of the mighty.

39

CONGRESS HALL

When our Colonial ancestors were not spending their time knocking off Indians and British and casting Liberty Bells they mainly shod horses, and wrought iron railings, foot scrapers, door knockers, gateways, fences and anything else you could twist out of a hot bar.

Then along came Progress and Machines and everybody went into tool and die cutting and lotsa money.

However, Philadelphians have not destroyed everything, only almost, and now that Independence Hall is sacred and restored, the railing over the entrance doorway to the Congress Hall will probably last a little longer.

On this balcony stood George Washington, William Penn, Benjamin Franklin, Betsy Ross, Abraham Lincoln, Teddy Roosevelt and General Figelmesyi, the Hungarian patriot who gave my Uncle Wilhelm a medal, and Richardson Dilworth.

The object of my affection is the balcony, however, and all its little wrought iron, or maybe they were cast iron friends, and it would do your heart good and also take off your weight if you just once walked around the Olde Colonial City and found a few remaining examples of the work of our crafty forefathers. Most of the better examples are now in dusty museums or have been boiled down for stuffed hand grenades, but Spruce and Pine Streets are par and the rail on the back of the old Customs House gives you five points.

The super-gate to the Pennsylvania Company (15th and Chestnut) is new. Samuel Yellin. 1936.

Happy Washington's Birthday!

1787

UNIVERSITY MUSEUM

The character for today is the late lamented architect Mr. Wilson Eyre. Wilson Eyre died about fifteen years ago and lived to see most of his work destroyed.

He was born in Florence, Italy, and spent his boyhood there and brought back to Philadelphia a romanticism which gave the old Colonial Dames a taste of antique polish and Tuscan charm. Most of it has gone, except for a few doorways and a couple of country houses and the one wing of the University Museum.

Of course it would be difficult to explain a character like Wilson Eyre nowadays because his eloquence and great ability were expressed by his drawings, which had personality and were translatable into brick, stone-carving, wood details, stained glass and the many other crafts which went into the making of a building.

Wilson Eyre's inspirations were European and his University Museum is derived, I think, from the "Last Supper" Church in Milan and the brickwork of Perugia, or was it the octagonal church in Bologna or that one in Ravenna? I forget. And perhaps the doorway is from, what was the name of that little town where the monks make a wonderful liqueur? But anyhow it's been a long time since I studied slides.

The thing about good Architecture, like any good Art, is the change of pace, and this is accomplished by the artist with variations in materials, play of lights and shadows with projections, cornices, thickness of jointing, textures and exotic marbles. If you want to see what our parents required of talented artists and artisans, sit in the cool shade of the cypress in the University Museum forecourt and try and count the number of things Eyre did to please the eye.

But of course that was all Bohemianism and today we are satisfied with a little aluminum here and a lot of glass there and the endless rah-rah blah-blah schmaltzy gabble that goes along with each concretion.

Eyre was a real architect. He not only could do pleasing elevations but also a good plan and an interior which has the Grand Manner. This is hard to explain to most people, who think anything higher than a seven-foot ceiling is not practical and hard to dust. However, the University with all its pomposity and Moderne approach still has sense enough to use the vaulted Auditorium and the beautiful Domed Room when it wishes to play host to royalty and minor firemen.

Located around the walls and subject to change without hurting the Museum Architecture is one of the world's greatest assemblages of the civilizations just preceding us, and in the dark recesses are living those charming gnomes who go off to the ends of the earth to bring back der Grospapa's bones and busted dishes.

When I was measuring the Sumerian shards at Khafaje one day (how's that for dropping names?) I kicked what I thought was an especially well-shaped stone and it turned out to be a small carved alabaster head with one shell eye and a lapis lazuli pupil. Did I pocket it? No, I catalogued it and cleaned it, and there it sits, beautifully mounted, behind glass, and for you to see, if you ever get your grandchildren or your wife to drag you to the University Museum.

BETSY ROSS HOUSE

Nobody in his right mind, except maybe me, would try to explain away the Betsy Ross House or the Betsy Ross legend, because Betsy Ross is a national heroine for snipping a five-pointed star out of a piece of folded muslin, right there before the eyes of George Washington, Benjamin Franklin and Baron Munchausen, in her parlor on Arch Street.

A lot of intelligent scholars and The Pennsylvania Historical Society and numerous enthusiastic Betsy Ross buffs have tried to find one shred of that Betsy Ross flag but so far have only come up with an ensign for the Pennsylvania Navy.

But outside of the wrangling of the thick-glasses scholar set, Betsy Ross seems firmly entrenched in the heart of America, and partic-ularly the Mayor's Committee for selling Philadelphia to the visiting yokels.

And as far as I am concerned, that is fine. I believe in Santa Claus, George Washington's cherry tree, the William Penn Treaty Oak, the Indian meeting ground in back of the old Ritz, the Letitia Penn House and Benedict Arnold's Mansion, all fine historical question marks.

Here is a drawing of what now is accepted as the Betsy Ross Flag House and I guess I'll have to fight for it. For more people take their wide-eyed children there and then send post cards to Enid, Oklahoma, to prove that they saw the room, and why spoil something that is sweet, lovely and gooey with just plain, dull facts?

MANAYUNK

Manayunk is that picturesque hill town on the other side of the Expressway. Now that Spring is just about here, the artists will soon be crawling around painting the place, which has already been made famous on the canvases of Francis Speight, the brothers Martino, Lucius Crowell and Walter Steumpfig.

It is in the 21st Ward, surrounded by West Manayunk and crowned by Roxborough. The most famous place is Proppers Furniture Store, which is where you were sent seventy years ago if you were an immigrant girl. There, you were tenderly reared and raised and taught English so you could marry some gentleman from your old village, who was being raised as a waiter in Stern's saloon and restaurant downtown.

Manayunk was the beginning of Siberia, which was a very common appellation mainly reserved for policemen who violated some of the sacred codes of the Department of Public Safety. After walking up those hills for a couple of years most cops earned the right to be called flatfoots. Now it's all red cars and the punishment is meted out somewhere else.

But mostly Manayunk is miles of hard granite—irregular, rough masonry relieved by white stone jointing. Life goes on mostly in the big mills, and tucked away in one corner is a very modern-looking playground. People used to get enough exercise just walking those hard hills.

If you know your way around, there are "the Blocks" and "Little Germany" and the closely knit groups of Italians and other minorities who live to be over eighty and remember the good old days when you had to walk up and down, instead of crowding the curbs with Cadillacs with good, steady brakes.

HAIL NORTHEAST
HIGH SCHOOL

Now that Mr. James Tate is Mayor of Philadelphia, let us look at his Alma Mater, Northeast (night). Old Northeast High School at 8th and Lehigh Avenues stands like the Rock of Gibraltar. Nearly everybody who reads, either went to Northeast or had to fight off Northeasters. Next to the Third Division which won the war, Northeasters are the great inheritors of High School Tradition and get tears in their throats at the very thought of "Whiff Whack Red and Black."

It's all much quieter now, since Northeast has been reduced to a coed school and moved uptown with trees around, and this old building on Lehigh has been renamed the Thomas A. Edison High School.

But the Northeast of Mr. Tate and other worthies was taught by the gentlemen of the hard collar, blue serge and vests and Phi Beta Kappa keys. They took no nonsense. You could study Latin and Greek, chipping and filing, sand moulding and casting, mechanical and free hand drawing, stenography and typing and a lot of other nuisances.

However, what I wish to direct your attention to is the Architecture of Northeast, for it is typical of the school architecture of yesterday, the Hard Stone Fortress; and old Central and old Southern, West Philly, Frankford and others were fenestrated similarly.

You entered through a glazed, massive entrance door in this cold, granite forbidding facade and were greeted by a wide staircase. You went to the basement lined with wooden lockers, reeking with the perfume of uneaten lunches, wet rubbers, damp overcoats and the thousand smells of boys, unventilated by air conditioning.

Around a central light court and four-story walk-up were the classrooms, opening on wide corridors with heroic figures in plaster. Mostly they were old Greeks, Pallas Athena and Hercules and the Laocoön group and all the others. The walls were adorned with brass plaques memorialising former classes, the windows were interlaced with stained glass fragments from former classmates. There was

a large dusty trophy case with partly deflated footballs with the winning score, yellowing baseballs, soccer balls and a lacrosse stick and cups beautifully engraved to the victors.

Northeast's patron saint is the late Dr. Andrew J. Morrison, who started teaching during the Civil War and lived to a ripe old age, holding the great respect of his students. They were mainly sons of Scotch weavers, Irish bricklayers, Italian masons, and small merchants. This was what produced great soccer teams, lawyers, doctors and Mayors. I owe a lot to Dr. Morrison. He discovered my talent and nursed it along. I visited his office regularly when I fell behind. The teachers got tired of poor examination papers, in ungrammatical English, but covered with drawings.

You never went to the front office if you could avoid it, because your father might be sent for. And if he had to come see the principal, he lost a half day's pay. That would always bring out the worst in parents.

But Dr. Andrew J. Morrison never sent for my father. He made me sit in the hall outside his office and study a large painting which was by Ot Schmidt and a memorial to his class. I was always completely embarrassed and never quite understood what it meant. In the center of the picture was a full size, realistically painted, red headed nude naked as a needle. She was holding straight out and looking into the Mirror of Truth. "Miss Northeast" was flanked by two kneeling nude figures about the size of tackles and they were offering the lady a beautiful steam locomotive and a lovely steamship. You can see that I really studied that picture when I should have been back in class studying my forty lines of Greek.

Well, here it is fifty years later and Dr. Morrison was right. While I have never been able to draw a presentable nude, I can draw a couple of other things. And when I was in Greece, the only thing I could say was "Good morning." But that was in pure, unadulterated, classic Greek with a Philadelphia accent. No Greek understood me.

READING TERMINAL

In 1923 Philadelphia lost by fire one of its greatest assets, the Pennsylvania Railroad train shed. (We got Penn Center instead.) The Pennsylvania train shed was built to be larger than the Reading Railroad train shed, and it won. It was the biggest aspidistra in the world and measured 300 feet wide and 108 feet, six inches high and 595 feet long.

Now, for the moment, Philadelphia still has the Reading shed, but I suppose it will soon be in the way of a parking lot or something, so you better hurry around and enjoy it while you may.

Of course, train sheds are not as picturesque without steam engines and wisps of smoke and very old conductors who wear vests with a turnip on the end of a chain for a watch, and punch tickets with fancy shots so you can't just sit there and make believe he already punched your ticket.

But maybe the Reading Co. doesn't deserve to have a beautiful, historic monument like the shed because they have done everything possible to board it up and hide it and keep you from seeing the train you are just missing, through those inflexible iron gates. Also, there used to be the best restaurant in Philadelphia with wonderful, ageless colored gentlemen who waited on tables and the counter and lorded it over everybody, including company Vice Presidents.

Beneath the vast shed remains that amazing market, full of beautiful smells of up-country Dutch goodness, meats, sea food, scrapple and Bassett's ice cream, and family-pride butchers and bakers and sugar-plum manufacturers. It is being antisepticised and cellophaned and generally cleaned up, but there is still the aroma of old times, which are probably better in memory.

Of course, nowadays, with electric trains and Diesel engines and everything clean and neat and ship-shape you don't need anything like a big beautiful room for a train shed, and so we are content with such efficient, charming, seven-foot subways as Pennsylvania Suburban, but how can I make a drawing of that?

THE DAIRY
(Mount Pleasant)

"Mount Pleasant, built by John MacPherson in 1761, is generally and justly regarded as the finest of the old houses of Philadelphia and indeed of all the northern Colonies," said the late Fiske Kimball, "Mr. Art Museum."

It just goes to show how little you can tell about what you are looking at, because I always thought it was the Arnold Mansion, and was where Benedict Arnold gave the British the secrets and escaped through a tunnel under the house and down to the Schuylkill right after he married Peggy Shippen and left her the house as a bridal gift.

I knew all this was so because for several summers my Uncle John and Tante Bertha ran a candy-pretzel-and-ice cream stand at the house to the left of the Mansion, and I spent many a summer walking to and from, and selling pretzels and peanuts to the sometimes-hungry spectators who were watching ball games in the surrounding territory.

They were only fairly interested in the Mansion. In fact, I really always thought it was called the Dairy. But I was not much of a historian—nor of a pretzel salesman, either, for at that time I was interested mainly in watching a sandlot pitcher named Zingy Zilensinger.

Since those faraway days of golden youth I have come a long way, and now look on the Mansion with awe and esteem and a certain lordly approach. The exteriors are majestic and the interiors are rich and the garden is superb and the furnishings are reminiscent of the glorious days of perukes, periwigs, embroidered waistcoats, candlelight, minuets and cold nights riding home from Fairmount Park in those unheated sedan chairs.

There is a chain of houses now, furnished by the good women of Philadelphia and squired by the Museum, and you could go see them if you really tried.

Take along a bottle of Wagner's Madeira and a crystal-clear, unwashed Waterford glass for the road.

SHIBE PARK

As long as I can remember, and that must be a hundred and forty years ago come last April first, the signs of spring were the Bock Beer goat which adorned the swinging doors of the corner saloon and the beginnings of the arguments about the merits of the Phillies and the Athletics.

The Athletics have moved to Kansas City, they tell me, and the Phillies have taken over Shibe Park and renamed it Connie Mack Stadium and put a standing figure of Mack in the park across the street, and they are about to move away, so farewell to the dear-to-my-heart scenes of my childhood, Shibe Park, which it was originally known as, and as far as I am concerned still is except it has changed.

Before progress and doubledeck stadiums and hieroglyphic scoreboards and night lights, the right and center-field wall was only as high as a white elephant's eye. Then, oh then, the two-story houses across the street rented their roofs to watch the World Series. If there was a crowd you could sit on straw out there on the edges of the outfield and a hit into the crowd was covered by ground rules which made it a two-bagger.

I guess it is all much better now except there hasn't been a hundred thousand dollar infield like Baker to Barry to Collins to McInnis, and nobody has hooked a slide into second base with all spikes and fists flying like Ty Cobb. Of course, those were all plays you could judge from a twenty-five cent seat in the bleachers on a hot sunny Saturday afternoon in August.

But the thing which has made baseball a more beautiful and bearable spectacle is the night game. Now you may sit in the cool of the evening under perfect lighting conditions and beautiful color, and thoroughly enjoy the greatest ballet art form ever invented by Americans, unless you believe the Russians invented "Beisbol".

I wouldn't tell anybody except my erudite readers this fact, because if there is anything Americans hate it is to be accused of being interested in Art; and also, it might be difficult to convince a fan that a well executed double play is as beautiful and poetic as a pas de deux by André Eglevsky and Maria Tallchief. The difference is that all you need to see lots of double plays are a blue shirt, a fog-horn voice and the patience to explain to your friend's wife what all the shouting is

about. On the other hand, to see Maria Tallchief and André Eglevsky requires white-tie-and-tails equipment and a hot auditorium in the middle of winter and the ability to keep awake while a guy in white tights is jumping through a window to get a rose.

To be a real baseball aficionado fan you must remember something you saw but hardly anybody else saw, which is easy if you go to Phillies games.

One I never saw—so I believe it—was about the guy who stole first base. It was Nick Altrock, who besides being a good ball player was also a comedian.

I may as well tell it my way, because the Sports Department will correct me anyway, but it seems that Washington needed a single run to win a game (a very rare achievement) and there was a man on third, one out, and Altrock was on second when who should come up but a rookie who couldn't hit the ball back to the pitcher.

Altrock signals for the boy to strike out. Then Altrock on second streaks back toward first, the catcher throws the ball to second to catch Altrock and the guy on third comes home standing up—and there is Altrock safe on first base. There is a loud rhubarb and everybody comes out of both dugouts and the umpires start getting the book out and Altrock says that it only says to move around the bases but it doesn't say positively only counter-clockwise.

Well, the Washington Senators won and right after that they changed the rule book so you may now only advance forward and not backward.

What I started to say was something about the architecture of Shibe Park, but I never really understood it myself, except that Connie Mack had an office in the tower. It is what we might term the false front, if you wish to be crude. What it is trying to do is simulate the Colosseum in Rome, or is it the Baths of Diocletian combined with a Barocco Roccoco icing of ornament and an interplay of brick and limestone with a heavy rustication on the lower story to give the effect of solidity. You would never know from just looking at it that behind that theatrical facade yawns a very large steel and concrete stadium where many people have gotten a sun tan hoping the Phillies would again win a pennant.

RICHARD SMITH
MEMORIAL

This being the One Hundredth anniversary of the Civil War—or was it last year—let us consider the Smith Memorial in Fairmount Park.

Mr. Smith left $50,000 to memorialize distinguished officers in the Civil War and also Richard Smith himself got worked into the design, even though I hardly think his services in the Civil War were that distinguished. What makes that point interesting to me is that Mr. Smith was a blacksmith and the only other blacksmith I ever heard of who got his picture painted was old Pat Lyon by John Neagle. This is in the Academy of The Fine Arts in case you wish to argue about portraits of blacksmiths.

I guess it has been fifty or sixty years since I shook hands with President McKinley, or was it Abraham Lincoln, I forget, but mostly I remember right now Mose McGovern's horseshoeing and wagon wheel and blacksmith shop which stood at Twelfth and Poplar Street right across from Grandmom's house. On Sunday afternoon as a special treat we could stand just inside the doorway and watch Mr. McGovern back into a horse and straddle its raised foot and pull off an old shoe and scrape the heel and heat a shoe until it was white hot and fasten it on the horses hoof and drop a hot poker into the water bucket. The aroma of burnt horses' hooves and steaming iron is right with me to this moment and it may be attar of roses to those who just read about these things.

But mostly I keep thinking of Mr. Richard Smith huffing on those bellows and pulling off horseshoes and piling up a fortune just to give a memorial to the City in memory of the Civil War heroes, and I am glad the architect found a big prominent wall for Mr. Smith's statue.

Well, the Smith Memorial was designed by John Windrim and twelve American born sculptors and sculptresses and is a fine example of what happens when you get cocky about being proud that it was all done by Americans because to my failing eye it is all inspired from Roman architecture and Classic sculpture and antique inscriptions.

In fact it all turns out to be a very undistinguished pile which you can't tear down and you can't plant out and you can't recommend to the young as an inspiration. In fact I guess the best thing in the whole deal is the statue of Mr. Richard Smith who looks as if he is enjoying being a rich old blacksmith turned type founder and completely solid bronze American.

Taken as an architectural ensemble it is no. But maybe if they got some of that sculpture down to eye level, it would look better. There's plenty of room in Fairmount Park and you could study Grafly's General Reynolds and French's General Meade and Ward's equestrian statue of General Hancock and Potter's equestrian statue of McClellan.

That's my suggestion for today but don't expect action.

Also, if you collect "echoes," the Smith Memorial has one of those embarrassing things where if you sit on one bench everybody can hear everything you whisper on the opposite bench.

57

ELLEN PHILLIPS SAMUEL
MEMORIAL

The Ellen Phillips Samuel Memorial is one of those gifts to Philadelphia which makes you wonder whether taxes aren't a much better way of getting dough from rich old ladies, rather than letting them have their way, as explained in the will drawn by a Philadelphia lawyer. This procedure only leads to expensive legal wrangling and the overstuffed courts have to decide what they think she really meant.

Ellen Phillips Samuel and J. Bunford Samuel were a fine Philadelphia-loving couple who looked like a daguerreotype of the court of Emperor Franz Joseph during the waltzing days of Vienna. If I remember exactly what my papa told me, it seems that while they were in Padua on a honeymoon they were rowed through a little canal which was lined with stone balustrades and there were little stone figures on the piers. Later, in the will-making years, Ellen Phillips Samuel remembered Padua in a haze of Italian moonlight, lavender and old lace and thought it would be lovely to have it all in Philadelphia and she left enough money to build it and a lot more.

I guess the great lawyer John C. Johnson must have drawn that will because it was as hard to break as his own will and caused an awful lot of artistic finagling and legal mumbo jumbo.

Mrs. J. B. Samuel's idea was to memorialize the history of the whole United States by having twenty sculptured figures of American history placed on stone piers with balustrades between the piers and all to be located on the East Bank of the Schuylkill between the boat houses and the Girard Avenue bridge. The final solution is not quite exactly what the will said, to a layman's way of thinking. For nobody could imagine so much "moola" being spent on so simple a solution. By the time Ellen Phillips Samuel was called to her great reward, nothing more tangible than beautiful architectural schemes had been completed. And these were of porticos and fountains, gazebos and benches, pools, tapis vertes, allées, pergolas and connecting walks and a sprinkle of sculpture.

By then Mr. J. Bunford Samuel was getting old and ruffled and he decided that if he hoped to see one figure completed for the Ellen Phillips Samuel Memorial, he had better commission it himself. This would surely set the style for all the twenty figures which would dot the east bank like a heroic-scale shooting gallery.

The first figure in American history, according to Mr. Samuel, was Thornfin Karlsefni, the Icelandic explorer who discovered the place. So J.B.S. went to Iceland and commissioned the noted Icelandic sculptor Mr. Einar Johnson to fashion a great statue of T.K., cast it in bronze and deliver the whole completed business to Fairmount Park. The sculptors, casters, base cutters and hauler unions massacred poor little generous Mr. J.B.S. for going out of the country and getting a foreigner, and they almost succeeded in not allowing the statue to land and be dedicated. J. B. Samuel gave up and hoped that the next hero would be commissioned by his heirs and match the beautiful heroic looking Thornfin Karlsefni. But no.

Samuel died and the whole subject lay dormant and collecting interest until the depression. Then Eli Kirk Price, who really ran Fairmount Park, decided that the time was ripe for stirring the dormant Samuel Memorial money. He commissioned Paul Philippe Cret, the noted Franco-American architect, to design the whole business.

Paul Cret worked out a very creditable scheme which is now complete and is fundamentally sound and could have been lovely. He didn't follow the will exactly, but he didn't completely ignore Mrs. Samuel's general idea.

Cret was an architect of Beaux Arts training which is now pooh-poohed. With Jacques Gréber he had designed the Parkway which he hoped would succeed with fine buildings and plantings and act as a gateway to Fairmount Park. There the flow would continue past the boat houses and the gracious Samuel Memorial.

It would consist of three large paved open

SPIRIT OF ENTERPRISE

spaces partly enclosed by large stone panels carved with historic inscriptions and around them the statues of the historic figures of the era. The three spaces were for the Early Period, the Middle Period and the Modern Period. Between the three were to be fountains and landscaping, trees, shrubs, benches and walks where you could enjoy history and the life on the river, just like Paris in 1880, complete with hansom cabs, barouches, landaus and lovely cocottes.

For all this, at various times, twenty-three sculptors have been chosen to execute a piece of American history. At first there were competitions, which took up the whole terrace of the Museum, and later the committee invited some of the name boys like the late Gaston Lachaise, Kooran der Harootian, Sir Jacob Epstein, Jacques Lipchitz, the late Waldemar Raemisch, Aaron Ben-Shmuel, José de Creeft and others.

With that international set sculpting away on American history you should expect the completed whole to be a great tribute to America, Mrs. J. Bunford Samuel, the Art Jury, the Fairmount Park Art Association and sculpture.

But here we find a most irritating collection of uninteresting examples of the work of outstanding men and women, most of whom have done much better elsewhere. The good group is Sir Jacob Epstein's. He ignored all the requirements and his work isn't on the river at all. By some legal maneuverings it sits up on the hill flanking the entrance to the Museum, and thank goodness.

If you don't mind getting killed by the traffic you really should go out to the Samuel Memorial and see what great inspiration the history of our country has been to twenty-three famous sculptors.

I guess the best thing about the Samuel Memorial is Cret's architecture. The great value of the architectural scheme is that now you can easily remove all the figures and relocate them in Fairmount Park or some of the little squares around Philadelphia or in Penn Center. Then we can start the whole thing all over again. There is still a lot of Samuel money and a whole new generation of sculptors who can get a cut.

PAOLI LOCAL

Philadelphia is bound on the West by the Paoli Local. Many people who use it treat Philadelphia as if it were a Colony of the Main Line, only to be visited for the Friday afternoon concerts of the Philadelphia Orchestra and Tuesday nights for the Metropolitan Opera (if it ever comes back). Otherwise most patrons boast that they never or hardly ever come into Philadelphia.

I guess the oldest, corniest, and possibly true story is about the Paoli regular who caught the eight-fifteen in and sat reading his New York Times every weekday for twenty-five years. And regularly, every weekday for twenty-five years, a gentleman sat in front of this passenger and read his copy of the Wall Street Journal. As the train approached Wynnewood, the Wall Street Journal reader would tear his paper into little pieces and waft them, slowly, out the window, until the shreds floated away, just before reaching the Suburban station.

After patiently watching this procedure daily for twenty-five years, our first commuter screwed up his courage and said to the occupant of the seat in front, "Sir, if you will pardon the intrusion, for twenty-five years now I have watched you, with great interest, tear your copy of the Wall Street Journal into little pieces and sift them out the window as we came into Broad Street Station. May I be so bold as to inquire why you do that?"

"Hrumpff, hrumpff," said the gentleman, "I do it to keep the Indians away from the Main Line."

"Keep the Indians away?" said the amazed questioner. "There hasn't been an Indian in these parts for over a hundred years."

"You see," said the Wall Street Journal reader, "it works, doesn't it?"

Well, what with the Roosevelt era, taxes and the winning of the West, the big estates have gone the way of Progress. What was formerly the hallowed domain of the Mighty Few is now the home of the quarter-acre-station-wagon-set. The only thing left of the Old Main Line is the awful unwashed aura of tweedy, wax-in-the-ears England.

Otherwise nice people who used to live alongside you in the center of the cosmopolitan city suddenly blossom forth in tartans which apparently are aged in compost heaps and come complete with matching bags, hats, and long, scratchy Scottish wool underwear.

And at some time or other during the day they manage to get a ride on the Paoli Local which encourages the aura by providing without question the oldest, crummiest and most uncomfortable cars in its already worn-out collection. Once in a while if you know the angles and can afford to sleep late, there is one luxurious-for-the-Pennsylvania Railroad, air-conditioned, Budd, stainless steel train.

And for a real strength of character test, ride the trains in and out when they are loaded with those monsters from "the playing fields of Eton," going and coming from their gentlemanly schools of learning. It's hard to believe that a beautiful china-blue eyed flaxen doll complete with English schoolgirl Peter Thompson outfit could outdo her equally well dressed brother in mayhem, but my advice is to keep your guard up.

Above is a picture of the Strafford station, and you better look quick. I think it is the last of the lovely wooden gingerbreads of the Victorian period. The new ones are those brick and concrete uglies which are indestructible but hardly worthy of a drawing.

61

THE AUCTION

This is a famous Philadelphia institution; the auction sale. When you see a red flag hanging outside a doorway in Portugal it means fresh meat in a butcher shop. When you see a red flag hanging out a doorway in Philadelphia it means "Auction Sale Today."

I don't believe I ever bought a thing at an auction sale which didn't seem too expensive at first glance, but later turned out to be a big bargain.

The dean of auctioneers is a Mr. Brickley whose eye is well trained to Philadelphia furniture and the Philadelphia antiques who buy bargains at auction sales. Just like horse people and dog people and cat people and bird people, there are auction people; not only regular people who love bargains but also dealers who know everything and can be trusted to get it for you at a slight extra. That, of course, is not half the fun of scratching your nose or nodding your head and finding that you have just bought a complete set of first-edition, unfoxed, uncut *Alice in Wonderland* for only $128,000 and a steal at that.

On the first floor is the minor league stand up sale, where you can still buy an ironstone pitcher and wash basin, only slightly chipped, or a perfect gem of a Victorian rocker missing only the wicker seat.

What every boy should know, outside of what he knows all about already, is how to sit patiently at an auction sale without raising his finger or moving his head, but watching future Rosenbachs, Sussels, Miss Zahns and other pros. From them he might learn how to spot a replate of Paoliuolo's *Battle of the Naked Men*, or a fake Rembrandt, or even how to sleep right straight through his wife's description of how she outwitted Brickley and got a genuine set of Lowestoft made for the Caliph of Bagdad and smuggled out by a knowing Armenian rug dealer.

But once I really did bid on what I thought was a leather-bound box of Franklin imprints. I got it for $12, but then it turned out I only got the boxes and nary a single imprint, which is worth about two million.

GERMANTOWN

GERMANTOWN, I love you . . . and all I can wish is that the City Planners stay down in Society Hill and leave you to enjoy your heritage and a few isolated examples of progress, you should please excuse the expression.

I guess it was wonderful when Op den Graeff and Pastorius and Rittenhouse arrived. But then George Washington set up housekeeping with the Continental Congress right after General Grant pushed him out of the Chew Mansion. He found the air salubrious, and so have a lot of other Philadelphians.

Well, here we are celebrating the 279th anniversary of the founding, so naturally I went back the other week to see if it was all still wide avenues and trees. It isn't all quite the same, but then neither am I.

Back there about 1864, Germantown Avenue was Main Street and there was Jimmie Jones for dry goods, Rowells for sixty-nine-cent shirtwaists, Darrow for hardware, stationery at T. D. Carson, Bieringles for hard candies, Harkinsons for chocolate eclairs, and Harpers for spooned-out ice cream if you brought the family cut-glass bowl, and Plet-chers for fine groceries with open bins of shelled almonds, ripe for stealing.

And the tennis matches with Bill Tilden and Suzanne Lenglen, Norris Williams, Bill Clothier, Borotra and Ichiya Kumagae. Cricket at Manheim watching Reynolds D. Brown and Jim Magill. Germantown Academy massacre of Germantown Friends, or was it the other way round?

Sleigh rides to Valley Green, Indian Head Rock and the beautiful monument to Pastorius in Vernon Park. Hurdy gurdies and hokey pokeys. The mess house and Cliveden. Louden, Carlton, Abbotsford Road and Fern Hill Park, Bob Riggs and his snakes and trains. The Germantown Boys Club and Cornelius Weygant. John Harbeson and his chess collection and the Society of the Jolly Grapefruit. Sunday afternoons at The Campbells playing croquet. Trolley cars, starched, white, long dresses and hair ribbons, ice cream pants and boater straws.

And Peace—calme, goode, olde, straightelaced Peace. Ah me, and I guess that entitles me to a free ride from Kirk and Nice.

The Perot-Morris-Deschler house is not so important architecturally, but it gained fame as General Howe's (British) headquarters. Then Colonel Isaac Franks owned it and he rented it to General George Washington who occupied it during the yellow fever plague in Philadelphia. Evidently anybody who could get out of Philadelphia during the plague came to the sweet air of Germantown and "discovered" the place. Now look at it.

Germantown Soldiers Monument in Market Square was erected by Ellis Post, GAR. If you think this corny, walk down the block and look at the horrors in architecture our generation is responsible for.

The Orpheum Theatre has been a fixture of Chelten Avenue and has a sort of Barocco Roccoco, wedding-cake encrusted, terra cotta architecture which is "Early Boom." It has survived stock companies, vaudeville and movies. Through its ornate portals have passed all "my sisters and my cousins and my aunts," getting a broad education before moving to the snootier airs of Chestnut Hill or the Main Line.

On West Walnut Lane: American Gothic, with the romantic quality of leaded glass, candlelight, and the rustle of petticoats to the accompaniment of the harp.

Germantown Mennonite Church, 1770, is typical of the dull general design of early Germantown houses—a random, unsurfaced, stone wall of a gray or black mica with gray limestone or mica jointing. The woodwork is simple and painted white, a white wood cornice and the pitch roof shingled with wood.

Fieldhouse of the Germantown Cricket Club. All that is left of the original property "Manheim." The clubhouse itself is a fine example of McKim, Meade and White architecture.

Early Twentieth-Century, retired-bankers',
Heidelberg, rusticated castle, bastard Gothic
crossed with sonofabitch German, complete
with towers, turrets, porte cochere and lace
curtains, dark furniture, dark oak woodwork,
dark and damp ugly.

VALLEY FORGE

Now is the time for all good men to take the family and a picnic lunch and go to Valley Forge where you haven't been for years. It's all changed, and much better than when you were a boy in knickerbockers.

The whole area is a beautiful, manicured park. The chapel is inspiring and beautifully designed. The ramparts are green. There are pieces of artillery, monuments, and a hundred antiqued log cabins spread around to make you feel proud of your heritage.

The outstanding architectural achievement is the monumental arch dedicated "to the officers and private soldiers of the Continental Army, December 19, 1777, to June 19, 1778." And within the arch is a quotation from Washington's notebook: "Naked and starving as they are, we cannot enough admire the patience and fidelity of the soldiery."

Since everybody and his brother is getting into the discussion of monuments and the architecture of monuments, the memorial arch at Valley Forge was designed by Paul P. Cret. The detail work was done by John F. Harbeson and was erected in 1914, just before Cret went to France to fight the First World War in the Infantry. You might say that it is inspired by the Arch of Titus in Rome, but the proportions and details are French Regency with a touch of Beaux Arts and a lot of early Cret. Architects then were still doing Roman Architecture and there does not seem to have been any fuss, only a lot of appreciation.

Well, here it is forty-eight years later and it still looks good like a memorial should.

If you wish also to argue about the Franklin D. Roosevelt Memorial problem down in Washington, I should say that a Roman inspiration is more modern than an inspiration from Stonehenge. Enclose a self-addressed stamped envelope with all letters. Thank you.

THE DEVON
HORSE SHOW

This is the sixty-sixth annual running of the Devon Horse Show and Country Fair, Incorporated. It is worthy of your closest attention and deserves a visit, or maybe several visits.

If you think that the horse is on the way out and is something to remember drawing your grandfather's brougham, go west, young man, at least as far as Devon and take a look at what care and pride can do to make the horse feel that all is not lost.

First I must say that a horse isn't just something you place two dollars on and close your eyes until it is all over. There are several kinds, and several species of each kind, and most of them are worth more than a box full of people who watch. And no horse at Devon is groomed as badly, or let us say as fashionably shabby, as the bluebones who saddle and mount them.

For while everybody loves to own and hang with blue ribbons a nice, clean, fresh, eighteen-hands championship single hackney horse, nobody but maybe a groom would appear in public with anything but a frayed derby and a habit which looks like it has bitten the dust of a thousand muddy jumps.

I, who cannot tell a descendant of a Godolphin Barb thoroughbred from a five-gaited saddle horse, am usually happiest walking around the perimeter where the stables are. There you can see beautiful harness and polished saddles and snaffles I guess you call it, and maybe hear some olde English as she is spoken. And usually seated on a fence is one of those beautiful, leggy specimens of golden-haired, blue-eyed American womanhood who can ride as if they are part of the horse and real purty, too.

Besides all the horse business there is a country fair where you may rig yourself out to look just as if you had one leg on the Devon Challenge trophy, or get your fortune told by a Wayne, Pa., gypsy, or just take a chance on a fur coat, Cadillac, and on down to a one-dollar kiss from a Bryn Mawr magna cum laude. It's all for sweet charity and high on the Social Register side.

What started as a nice little area event sponsored by the late, lamented "Ike" Clothier and a small group of devoted sportsmen has now grown to an international meeting with horses and horsemen assembling in the last week of May.

So come, oh come to Devon.

BRYN MAWR
GRADUATION

Here it is June already, and just when it's lovely outdoors, everybody and his parents have to swelter indoors through Graduation. The great intellects you suffered with for four expensive years suddenly appear in most dignified black robes with flowing sleeves and colorful cowls. And under a most unbecoming tasseled mortar board cap stands your darling, bathed and photogenic.

The locale of this scene is Bryn Mawr College. You can tell by the Cope and Stewardson Collegiate Gothic towers, turrets and mediaeval flags. They, of course, have graduation outdoors.

Last time I went to Bryn Mawr was to pick up an old Irish gal named Bowen. We hit a couple and had a fine time, and I finally deposited her back at the beanery or is it deanery. It was all correct.

If you are quite smart, Bryn Mawr will mold you. After four years you come out with your Philadelphia accent replaced by a Welsh brogue, and competent to argue with your peers, take an active part in goodness and be generally ready to meet the steel-rimmed glasses intellectual set.

Bryn Mawr is one of the three Quaker-founded colleges, and it rests comfortably on a Welsh tract. It is comparatively young, 1885. The College cheer is in Greek, of course, and goes *Anassa, kata, kalo, kale, ia, ia, ia, nike. Bryn Mawr, Bryn Mawr, Bryn Mawr,* whatever that all means.

It's all high class and no foolin' or fun. Years ago they used to have a rousing good May Day with just everybody dressed Greek and galumphing around the Maypole, white oxen with fillets and much hoopla in a refined, high-pitched way, and certainly not like the carryings on of the Greeks I have seen celebrating in Pompeii. But World War II killed all that nonsense and all is quiet and no Rowbottoms, goldfish eatings or any other spring riots so dear to the hearts of normal college students.

Nobody interesting like Elizabeth Taylor, Annie Oakley, Lydia Pinkham or Jacqueline seems to have graduated. From what I can find out everybody who ever graduated is really outstanding. Well, all right, like Kathryn Hepburn, Marianne Moore, Emily Kimbrough, Cornelia Otis Skinner and Katharine McBride.

The extent of political activities on the campus seems to be limited to a few invited Senators, and certainly no pinkos, Birchers, or Commies to disturb the minds.

One hundred and sixty out of a school of a thousand will graduate this year, and even though he won't get an honorary degree, guess who is going to deliver the address: no less than The Honorable Joseph Sill Clark, Senator from Pennsylvania, and besides a plug for himself I hope he says something nice about the candidate for Governor, his old pal, Richardson Dilworth, who could use a hundred votes.

Well, a doff of my mortarboard to all graduates and I hope they will run the world at least as well as we have.

How was that again, *ia, ia, ia, Bryn Mawr, Bryn Mawr, Bryn Mawr.*

WEDDING RECEPTION

Nothing is more pleasant, in June, than getting a few of those Caldwell or B. B. B. double-envelope engraved invitations to weddings and a reception at the home of the bride.

I shall confine myself to the reception, which is now a wonderful institution supplanting the big dinner with lots of toasts and speeches.

I love wedding receptions (in case you believe that I don't like anything). A proper reception now demands, first, a polished one-ring circus tent. It is strung up on a well-groomed lawn and surrounded with all the impedimenta of good caterers. Big trucks, groaning with boxes of fine foods, linens and napery, polished silver and an array of ancient waiters like you don't see many of nowadays around these parts any more. I think they must all be sons and grandsons, trained by Augustin and Baptiste, and are worthy successors to their forbears and Brillat-Savarin.

June wedding receptions are the climax of a long era of preparation, rehearsals and ceremony and trying to remember Aunt Hattie's second-marriage name, and that long, hot ride from the church, way down there, to the home way out there, and on a road which is not on the map.

Finally, there you are. The tent looms ahead the attendant takes your car and gives you an octagonal paper check which you won't ever be able to find again.

The long wait to greet the bridal party is relieved by a washer of cold champagne, which disappears quickly in the hot sun and needs constant refilling.

Well, at last, there is the line. You kiss everybody, the bride, mothers, sisters, aunts and a fine leggy collection of identical bridesmaids, and out you go on a fast trot to the main tent.

It seems that everybody else has gotten there ahead of you and the place is in an overheated, champagney uproar. It looks like the New York Company of My Fair Lady, everybody onstage, ready for the "Ascot Gavotte" number.

After all you have gone through to reach this heavenly moment, it is only fair and reasonable that you forget your reducing pill, breathe deeply of the stifling tent air, close your ears to the Bacchanalian racket and fully enjoy the fruits of the vine, and the field and stream and barnyard.

So, there you go, full glass in hand and plate in the other, loading it with chicken salad and chicken a la king, sliced Virginia ham and turkey and rare roast beef, fried oysters and shoestring potatoes and potatoes Anna, French peas and fresh asparagus, croissants and Melba toast. And then a scoop of coffee ice cream and a scoop of raspberry sherbet and salted almonds, ladyfingers, petit-fours, chocolate squares, and eclairs, cream puffs and white iced oblongs. And washed down with a fine Courvoisier or a B and B and maybe a taste of Armagnac and a soupçon of Anise, kimmel or goldwasser. And, of course, a long fine panatella and maybe a taste of the wedding cake, and a little box of cake to sleep on.

The music rises to a deafening pitch, the bride cuts the cake and everybody lifts still another toast. And just as you are going back for seconds with a beautiful much-too-young blonde, who should find you but your very own lovely wife who gently takes your arm and leads you through the crowd to the "thank you maams," the car and the sleepy ride home.

ROBIN HOOD DELL

To save myself and my more intelligent readers from nasty letters about me and what I dislike, which seems to be everything in and about Philadelphia, today I shall be complete and solid sweet.

Let us consider Robin Hood Dell, the outdoor music lovers' sylvan bosque. This gift of the city to the endurers of Philadelphia Summers owes its existence to the unceasing efforts of a supercharged Mr. Fredric Mann. In his own inimitable way he has convinced two thousand stay-at-homes to match the City Fathers in dividing the cost of maintaining the most extravagant and polished music season in this country.

The Robin Hood Dell concerts have risen from an informal, soothing, restful evening of Strauss, Gershwin, Victor Herbert and Tschai-kowsky mit real cannons and a sort of proving ground for grassroot conductors. Now it is the sacred grove of Stokowski in black tails and on down. But there is plenty of room for all possible approaches to listening to summer music from the white linen coat sponsors down to the blanket-on-the-ground, blue jeans pimple set.

The architecture of the sounding board is something I am glad it is one of my good days so I can't be anything but joyous about. I wish I could recommend something to gay it up. And I am glad I don't have to be wrapped around a cello in the hot morning sun, rehearsing under that concretion.

Well I've been kind and generous long enough and I will now go out and get a pickle sandwich and tune in *liebestod*.

OFF TO CAMP

Just about this time comes that lull in the day's occupation which is known as the "children are-leaving-for-camp" hour.

Unless you have to catch a train to go to Grandmom's funeral on that day, knowing travelers stay clear of the 30th Street Station, for there is just everybody and his children pack-jammed around Indian signs with their second-hand baggage, just good enough for camp.

If you ever left home to go into the Army, you could not have enjoyed a more tearful farewell than this one, to a bunch of spoiled brats leaving for a paradise somewhere too far to reach by less than a sleeper jump, but not too far away to be reached by mail, CARE packages and expensive long-distance calls to come and approve taking out the appendix.

I went to a camp one day, once, to visit. All I remember is a lot of unruly Indians paddling expensive canoes. And tennis experts and baseball giants. And lots of artsy-craftsy, pyrographic ruining of good leather and birch, and hard-to-get-rid-of clay models of practically everything.

Not being a parent or even a grandparent and never having had a childhood I wouldn't understand, but I really do. I have seen worn and torn parents sink into a Martini with that relief which surpasseth all understanding, once the dear ones are packed off to the cool North woods. Poor mom and pop have to stay right here in the air-conditioned city, worried the whole time what little Archimedes is doing or what more he will bring home than a Merit Badge for Art, two rattlesnake skins, a live frog and a hand-carved totem pole much too large for the apartment.

Well, only eight more years and he will be in Haverford and she will be in Bryn Mawr and then there will be nothing to worry about except girls, and boys.

PICNIC ON THE FOURTH

I know the Fourth of July is much better now and fewer kids die of lockjaw on the Fifth from having been burned by a whole package of Canton Midgets going off in their hands. Also I realize that it is safer and saner not to tamper with squibs, Roman candles, pinwheels, fountains, sparklers, punk, torpedoes, caps or giants.

Myself, I read the Declaration of Independence and sit in a captain's chair with a Martini in one hand and a twenty-two in the other and fire at a spinning target so I don't have to get up and change the birds. That is the advantage of middle age: you don't have to bend over and light dangerous firecrackers, you can just sit and make as much noise and live as dangerously.

Fourth of July is a sort of opening wedge for the summer picnic and it has come a long way in efficiency. When I was a boy it just seemed that Mrs. Feigenbaum and Mrs. Gottlieb and my Mother vied with each other to see who could make more jars of potato salad, pickles and mayonnaise, devil hard-boiled eggs, pile up rye bread sandwiches, cut up perfectly good fruit into salad, pack pretzels and salted potato chips, boil washtubs of coffee for the long haul to Willow Grove for the picnic.

By the time all that was consumed and appreciated the kids were sick, the men had retired to pinochle and the women were relaxing and quietly nursing their offspring and enjoying a moment of peace and quiet before the fireworks display and the finale, the "Teddy Roosevelt Attacking San Juan Hill" spectacular.

Now the stillness of the cool morning air is broken by the rumble of motors and exhausts. The caravan of station wagons arrives and the rears open to disgorge enough safari equipment to track down the Abominable Snowman. None of this peasant stuff of potato salad and rye bread sandwiches. There are portable outdoor grills, tents and swings, mattresses and easy chairs, boats, televisions and radios, phonographs, cameras and sporting gear. The costumes are the simplest and most abbreviated. The air reeks of insect creams, powders, potions and sunburn lotions.

The food is frozen, diet-measured, fat free, pure and sprayed against gnits and gnats and flies, fleas, mosquitoes and other deleterious matters. And then it is burned to death on crematory outdoor grills and served on plastic plates which are hard to burn up.

By the time it is all consumed and appreciated, the kids are sick, the men and women have retired to bridge, and suddenly somebody says Happy Fourth of July and let's get the show on the road.

PLAYHOUSE IN
THE PARK

There are lots of things about the John B. Kelly Playhouse in Fairmount Park which are worthwhile. To get to it you should drive out of hot Philadelphia and along Belmont Plateau, and around the circle to Belmont Mansion, one of the architectural gems of this country. The terrace is a wonderful place to dine and watch the sun go down.

Fairmount Park is still the seat of barbarism, a dry desert in wet Pennsylvania. So that if you wish to wine and dine like a civilized man, you must take along your private hip flask or a bottle in a paper bag like in Texas.

Up the hill in a bosky grove sits the Playhouse, a lovely setting and a relief from the baking pavements.

Some of my best friends and pass-giving theatre cronies get their summer sunburns pumping for publicity at the Playhouse and generally behaving as if sunlight and fresh air were things they were accustomed to instead of the winter nights in unkempt pressrooms.

There is a beautiful, characteristic, heroic-sized sculptured head of Jack Kelly at the entrance to the Playhouse. It is the work of the sculptor Mr. Reginald Beauchamp.

The summer-theatre set gets all dressed up for the evening and while they are mostly old first nighters, they don't expect Sarah Bernhardt or John Barrymore every week. There is iced organeade and root beer, and there is plenty of room for parking.

Theatre in the Round is something which was invented in Mexico where everybody stands around a table on which a beautiful senorita dances a bolero on the rim of a sombrero to the accompaniment of a single guitar. From these humble beginnings it has been blown up to tent-show size and you must be patient and appreciate the limitations and realize the many staging problems and consider that it's summer and it will be cooler when they get air conditioning.

I guess it is best for musicals where you don't care if you see or hear anything. But for those deeply significant jobs you should close your eyes, because the principals speak to you one second and turn their backs on you the next and even I can't quite get the nuances. At that point you realize that it would all be clear if you had only taken that third Martini.

About the architecture of the permanent shell, don't expect a Baroque Festspiel house of gay old Vienna, complete with gilded ornament and flying plaster angels and towers, turrets, gee gaws and chichi, flags, lanterns and everything else which used to denote summer, fresh air, heady amusement and Fledermaus joy.

No, no, the place is Modern (1880 laminated wood arches), grim and dipped in Grand Rapids fumed-oak shellac.

But if you wait outside for that last plaintive call of "curtain going up," and follow the usher's flashlight in the darkness, the gloomy interior won't irritate you and ruin your high spirits.

FISHING IN THE SURF

If you want to be a surf fisherman you must play the game and live at least sixty miles away from the ocean. Then, oh then, you can rise in the middle of the night and tiptoe around noisily, waking the whole family. There is nothing like hot coffee at 4 A.M.

The car is loaded and smelling to high heaven of old oilskins, boots, leather gloves, rod cases, rotting bait, rusted tackle boxes and two hoagies wrapped in newspaper.

You are off in the cold morning on the fast drive through empty Jersey roads. The meadows chill you. You reach the beach, set up your rod holder, dump your equipment, bait the line and heave it out toward Spain.

Ah, the joy of it all! The wind whips your shirt, the salt water rides over your boots, the gulls hover over your bait. A tug on your line and a tightening of the thread and a slight rise in blood pressure. It's gone and you haul in and bait again, and cast and bait and cast. The sun comes up and warms you, the sun stays up and burns you. The sun goes down and you fold your tents and silently steal away to the nearest fish counter and buy a couple for mom and the kids.

One day when I was in New York, I went up to the fish department of Abercrombie and Fitch and I asked for the man who answered all the damfool questions about fish. He leaned back in his chair and put down the line he was tying to catch a whale and said would you like to fish off the Grand Banks for tuna, or we have a party going to Portugal to play the wily herring. In Alaska we can set a camp of sure salmon and maybe we could get you in on a tarpon party off the Bahamas.

Look, said I, I am a little dope living near a quiet stream and right away everybody says what you need is trout. Now what I would like is a bamboo pole with a long string and a bent pin which wouldn't hurt a fish.

Well, he said, I will tell you what to do. You turn right as you leave my office and take the elevator down and never come up on this floor because once you ask a salesman out there what to buy he will load you with enough stuff to ruin fishing for any lover like yourself.

Sir, I said, I cannot thank you enough but ain't you supposed to sell fishing? The gentleman gave me a sweet look and said I organize parties and I take fishermen out and I pull the things in but actually I hate fish. If there is a ham sandwich within a quarter mile I wouldn't touch the finny things.

A HOUSE IN
THE COUNTRY

This is a Pennsylvania farmhouse, so dear to the heart of every wife with a couple of bucks and a yearning to "get away from it all" and live the simple rustic life like a horse or a flower or a peasant.

To be a real Pennsylvania farmhouse, like you don't see many of nowadays, it should have a view all the way to Lancaster, a stream and a swimming hole without algae, mud, or your husband's sister's noisy children. Also fruit trees which bloom without care, dogwood and a garden which looks lovely with everything out. A garden is a swell place to wear tight pants and big hats and Paris gloves just to cut a couple of rare pansies or a very special trained wild orchid or ladyslipper.

There you can relax your aching back on a white iron chaise longue and look for the hundredth time at robins or bluebirds through special binoculars which are strong enough to see to Spain, and of course mostly you see only starlings and sparrows who live in the country all day and go in on the Paoli Local to annoy the city folks all night.

A good solid farmhouse should have that beautiful rotten stone, laid quaint and exposing termited beams, creaky, stocking-ripping floors, rusted plumbing and leaky window frames. That will give Pop something to do over weekends, just when he is dreaming of watching a ball game or sneaking off into the poison ivy to catch a few winks before the visitors descend all full of fresh air and ready for a couple of long gin-and-tonics and dull family talk.

Or a whole flock of visitors making like a painting by Pieter Brueghel and partying up the place with paper plates and paper cups and paper napkins and Coca-Cola caps, beer caps, cigarette butts and the rest of outdoorsy enjoyment which makes Monday morning so irritating.

But the catch is still to find a farmhouse which isn't surrounded by some son-of-a-builder's idea of suburbia with ranch houses perched up on your view or looking into your master bedroom window, or wrecking the quiet air with the squalling of their noisy brats.

Maybe it is better you should stay in town and not drive over the weekend. There you can dream your dreams with a fresh copy of the Sunday Bulletin Magazine over your face and a drink in a glass to comfort you. And also, your chances of being alive on Monday are better.

90

WEEKEND SPECIAL

Ever since Henry Ford invented the automobile (or was it the Russians?) weekends are something to rest up for all week.

Friday is that day which clockwatchers look forward to, and as soon as the gong sounds they drop their picks and race for home and mama and the kids, load up the car and head for the shore.

That leaves the city lover two full hot days to love the city in peace and quiet, air-conditioned comfort with uncrowded movies and restaurants, band concerts and just plain settin' and eatin' and drinkin' and sleepin'.

But after a couple of months of complete comfort the call of the wild waves gets into your wife, or somehow you can't get out of an invitation and down you go with the peasants.

Hotel rooms being hard to get for just middle-aged weekenders, you content yourself in a hot double room right under the kitchen, with all the plumbing exposed and noisy at 6 A.M. So you might as well get up and enjoy early morning on the beach with naught but fishermen, seagulls and a couple of roving delinquents for company.

By high noon you are burned and miserable and smelling oily and sandy. By nightfall you are mosquito-bitten and loaded with too many Martinis to take away the sudden chill. By midnight you are sick of people you wouldn't send a Christmas card to, and by Sunday morning you have had it and hope the noon cocktails and dinner party will drop you into the front seat, relaxed and sleeping like a baby while your wife drives home because you drove down.

Once I decided to make a list of all the things which are absolutely necessary for solid comfort at the seashore. But instead, I drew it above so the insurance company couldn't complain if I claimed a lost left sneaker. But what I did lose was the keys to the trunk.

93

THE FERRY

Since this column has become a sort of geriatrics Wailing Wall, let me cry over the passing of the Philadelphia-Camden ferries.

Anybody who is old enough to remember citronella, bathing suits with tops and salt water taffy had to cross the Delaware on the ferry, unless he walked across on the ice.

I know it's all corny now, but I'm corny and paid to be. The ferry was the opening and closing event of the one-dollar Sunday excursion to Atlantic City and worth it, if only to ride the fastest train in the whole world. And a very pleasant way to get enough sunburn to last all summer in the city.

For the excursion set, which we were, the day started at 5 A.M., and hot. By 5:30 we had to catch the trolley which would get us down to the foot of Market Street by 6:30.

There is nothing to equal the memory of the ferry house, and thank goodness. At 6:30 A.M. it was a cool interior reeking with the left-over aroma of horses, farmers, wagons, hot dogs and popcorn, fishermen and their smelly gear, oil, ropes, empty chicken crates and a milling crowd of parents and their half-fare offspring.

To properly appreciate the ferry you had to get there early and press against the iron gates which separated you from the river. As the boat approached, the crowd would suffocate you and the boatmen would push everybody aside to unlatch the big wheel, pull out the thick ropes and get ready to tie her up.

The sides of the slip were lined with a barrier of tree trunks all corded together, which acted as a pad. No ferry captain in his right mind would come right up to the slip without hitting the logs and bounding over to the other side and hitting them, too, for luck.

This maneuver sounded like the screech you let out when you catch your finger in a door, or the moan and groan of I don't remember what except a ferry slip.

From then on there was a musical serenade of the big wheels tightening on the ropes, the toot of the ship's whistle, the clanging of the gates and the pitch of the boatmen to "letem-off." Finally the horses and wagons, early automobiles and trucks and sleepy passengers were gone, the big gates would swing open and you could run to the front of the boat and press against the rail.

In the cool of August with a breeze away from the League Island dumps you could imagine you were out at sea. Well for maybe ten minutes. Then a repeat of the landing performance and there ahead lay the rear lights of the excursion train.

About 10 P.M. the excursion train would return, and half-asleep you would be dragged through the dank ferry house to the waiting boat and crammed up against the rail to admire Philadelphia at night. But what with the gentle rocking of the boat and the cool breeze, I can't exactly remember what caused my woozy feeling. Maybe too much sunburn or the brown paper wrapping on Mama's sandwiches or the popcorn, peanuts, hot dogs, spun candy or forbidden crab cakes, or maybe the endless merry-go-round, but most likely the returning fishermen with their overheated catch.

Anyhow when it was over you could ride home in the trolley and sleep the deep sleep of the weary but relieved traveller.

Now, of course, you whirl across the Delaware bridges where the rails are too high to let you enjoy anything.

95

THE ART MUSEUM

The Philadelphia Museum of Art sits, like the Parthenon in Athens, on the crest of a hill overlooking the city, but the comparison stops there.

Let us say the architecture is of Greek inspiration—maybe Attic Greek. It is late Corinthian with a lot of color and other deleterious matter added and about twice as big as anything Greek.

A short course in Architecture and the other minor fine arts is that in Classic Architecture and Art (which now is considered bad taste, of course) you put on everything you knew, and in Modern Architecture and Art you know everything and leave almost all of it out; and it, of course, is wonderful. Now that you have passed the course we proceed back to the Museum on the Parkway.

There were many doughty Philadelphians and a couple of Frenchmen like the late Jacques Gréber and Paul Cret involved in getting the Museum to fruition, but mostly it is there because of the late Eli Kirk Price. The gentleman who finagled all the Art within was a Boston bully boy, Fiske Kimball. He died a few years ago and now the place is run by two capable characters, Henri Marceau and Carl Zigrosser, and that "peace which surpasseth all understanding" has settled upon the Museum and thank goodness for quiet.

There are only about three things around here which have national importance—the Orchestra, the Barnes Foundation and the Museum. The Orchestra is sold out and you have to go to school to properly enjoy the Barnes collection, but the Museum is free and easy.

Now you can get a bus to take you out and bring you back. And while the food, served on the terrace, is nothing which the Cordon Bleu would copy, you can get a snack and sit in the open air and look out toward City Hall which does not ruin your appetite from way out there.

To go back to the exterior for a brief moment, if you look up in the pediment to the North there are a lot of highly colored Greeks in imperishable polychrome terra cotta symbolizing "Art" or something equally incomprehensible, and sitting obscure and alone in a basement are the figures for the South pediment, just waiting for Council to appropriate the money to raise them to their final resting place.

I might add, as a last word, that it would be instructive if you looked up and around. The architecture is full of akroterae, griffons and gazelles, bronze rings for swags and garlands, curved stylobates and a fine display of refinements, double entasis and optical illusions which would do the heart good of a student of Dynamic Symmetry. But to get to all this hidden charm you gotta climb fourteen hundred steps.

If you have any sense and an inactive coronary occlusion, take a taxi or drive to the rear entrance where there are only three steps, flanked by Rodin's "Burghers of Calais" and Epstein's "Social Consciousness."

The interior of the Museum is something else again and very worth while.

THE ZOO

When an American goes to Paris, what he wants to do most is go to the Folies Bergere, but when a Frenchman goes to Paris what he wants to do is go to the Vincennes Zoo (says la Poll Gallup).

When my father first came to Philadelphia in 1776, olde style, he met my mother and took her to the Zoo and bought her a yellow chrysanthemum and right there they became engaged. It was Thanksgiving Day and ever after on Thanksgiving Day we went to the Zoo. It was always cold and uncomfortable crossing the Girard Avenue bridge in damp corduroys in the November evening.

I guess I should like zoos because the other day my cousin told me that my great-grandfather was a bear trainer in old Transylvania. But I really can take zoos or leave them alone, and I have taken a good many of them, including Guatemala where they have a bulldog in a cage marked "Canine, America North."

It is real classy to like the Philadelphia Zoo and you should contribute because some day you will have grandchildren who get palmed off on you once a year and you can let them

run wild at the Zoo, and maybe be eaten by a tiger.

The Zoo sits on the tract which was once John Penn's country seat, "Solitude," and Penn's beautiful mansion is occupied by the Zoo's offices. At various times Philadelphia Zoo architects have designed buildings and they are as worthy of serious study as the animals. But who wants to look at architecture when you can watch a couple of monkeys embarrassing everybody?

The trouble with Zoo animals and me is that they are not caricaturable. If you give the average Homo Sap even a short rope he will naturally work into a caricature of his former self. But Zoo animals are always graceful and mostly beautiful and they never make a bad line, except, of course, maybe sometimes monkeys who are usually showing off, making caricatures of people.

This drawing, by the way, is of the entrance pavilions, Furness and Hewitt, Architects. Next year they will have been standing exactly one hundred years, which is some sort of record of achievement in these parts for a building which is not Colonial Architecture.

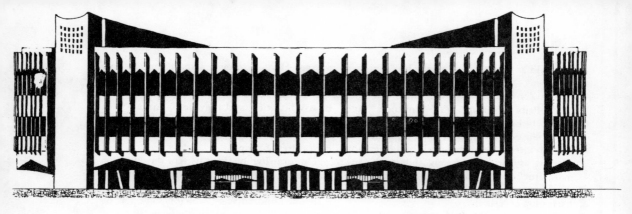

BAPTIST HEADQUARTERS

The new national offices of the American Baptist Church are now completed, and you may go have a look.

If you don't mind getting killed on the Sabbath by traffic, you head out the Expressway toward Valley Forge and pass new, architecturally undistinguished factories and offices which line the roads to the Turnpike. Right near the entrance, alongside a most ungodly new government missile plant, is the new home of the Baptists.

It is what I will call the Baroque period of Modern Architecture. It is basically a four story circular building with semi-circular radiating buildings, and I guess you could say as a point of arguing in favor of Expressionism that it looks Baptist.

I say that merely because it saves me from the wealth of clichés which are already old-hat. It has been called an inspiration from the Colosseums in Rome, Nimes, Arles, Timgad and Verona; but you know what happened in those Colosseums, hardly a fit inspiration for a Baptist Headquarters. It is also supposedly inspired by bull rings at Seville, Ronda, Madrid. Imagine! Anyhow, if you just look at it without any Baedeker encumbrance, it is a handsome solution and you can see it in the full round from your car window.

The architect of the buildings is Vincent Kling, a Dapper Dan who came to Philadelphia a few years ago and has practically rebuilt the old crumble almost single handed. He has won more medals, prizes and encomiums than all the architects around put together, and his chief charm is that you can enjoy his architecture without the wordy mumbo jumbo explanations accompanying the Looney set masterpieces.

HORSE PLAYERS

Like almost everybody, except maybe sixteen zillion people, I know betting on anything is wrong and wicked and some day I wish I could get up enough courage to go down to the window and place a two-dollar bet on a horse just to win, and not also to place and show.

One man I know bet on every horse every day. He told me once when he was down with a high fever in the Philippines he woke up and he was on a stretcher in the grandstand of a track. When he turned his head, there he was lying across the finish line.

So he called to an orderly and said, "I must have an awful high fever but am I really lying in the grandstand of a race track?" The orderly said he was lying in the grandstand of the race track at Manila because there weren't enough ambulances.

"Well," my friend said, "I can see from where I am lying that I am across the finish line and please do me a big favor and move my stretcher back because I never finish better than third."

In my line of work you meet up with a lot of people who do strange things, like golfers and fishermen, and in their spare time spend a lot of money and wind up getting just fresh air for their troubles. Horse players are some of them.

Except that horse players seem hardier than most outdoorsiers. The only investment is a pair of pawn-shop spyglasses and a pencil and maybe a long pin to punch through the program, and also a straw blonde to cry on if you lose or hug if you just happen to win.

Besides, horse players eat well and are better sports. It's a rare joe who works his way down the slot to throw a couple of boos at the jockey just because he didn't boot his bet home. No, you takes your choice and pays your money and by the time you tear up your ticket the windows are open again and the lead ponies are taking the horses around to the starting gate and "They're off" and there you are again booting in "Jojobo" with Bill Hartack or Willie Shoemaker up.

RITTENHOUSE SQUARE

I guess you should hurry around to Rittenhouse Square because one more large apartment house and you'll have to use a flashlight to see the fountain on a sunny day.

Actually it gets better with geriatrics from wall to wall and the dear boys leading around a fine collection of groomed canines with bad manners.

Rittenhouse Square goes back a long way and as free and easy as it is to get in now, that is how difficult it used to be, what with a high barbed iron fence and locked gates and nobody allowed except Philadelphia Firsts and their Nannies and hoops from Schwartz's toy store at Ninth and Chestnut. There was a cop in a high gray helmet and two cast-iron fountains spurting from long beaked cranes and everything was love-lly.

Then along came a character named Dr. J. William White who, while we wouldn't say he was quite an A.D.A. Liberal, was an early-do-gooder.

He got the iron fence down and had Paul Cret lay it out something like a Parc Monceau with a beautiful fountain, groomed trees, pebbled walks and fancy flower holders. Dr. White got a bronze portrait in memory and also a private sort of a walkway directly across from the stuffy Rittenhouse Club, so he wouldn't have to cross at the corner like the hoi polloi.

In addition there was founded The Rittenhouse Square Association with interlocking directorate and little silky old ladies who care. At Nineteenth Street there was a watering fountain for horses and I think it is now reduced to a bubbler.

I guess you are all ready now for a book list. So you can read all about it in *Rittenhouse Square* by Charles J. Cohen, a distinguished Gentleman and onetime President of the Rittenhouse Club.

PENNSYLVANIA DUTCH

Some nice weekend if you want to get away from it all, and you are skeered of the Turnpike, drive out through the Park and on to the back roads that lead to the Dutch Country which is roughly between Norristown, Bethlehem, York and Harrisburg.

The Pennsylvania Dutch are not Dutch at all, but are descendants of immigrants who came here before the Revolution, from Germany, Switzerland and Alsace. They are differentiated by religious beliefs, customs, courtesies, food and general deportment and the area must be seen to be believed.

With all the advances of civilization and inventions you would think that they would move out of the "horse and buggy, beards and sunbonnets age." But no, maybe it is better that way, finding somebody who maintains a calm, unruffled composure despite the advances of the "new frontier" salesmen.

If you think they are just backward hicks, however, do not trust your supposedly superior college knowledge in horse trading, cow bargaining or the selling of tobacco. They're smart. Somewhere back there they built the Conestoga wagons which preceded the prairie schooners and also forged the misnamed Kentucky rifle which helped win the 1776 war.

Right now they are having a run-in with the Government over the right to omit paying some taxes, because they take care of their own old and young and settle juvenile delinquency, if any, in their old fashioned successful way.

I am not one to belittle the advantages of piped hot water, station wagons or television, and I think canned and frozen foods beat all hollow anything Mother ever made. And besides, I am on a diet so all I can do is dream about Shoofly Pie, Schnitz un Knepp, Boova Shenkel and Rivel Soup, gastronomic delicacies which make a rugged Amish farmboy push away the dinner table, put on his flat-brimmed hat, mount his single man's black carriage and go over and court the neighbor's plump daughter.

Their "King's English" is something I wish I had made up, and the names of the small towns are sure-fire sophomoric gags which I can't print here but you can find them on any gasoline station road map.

Of course the whole area is haunted by the gimcrack dealers in baubles and imitation Dutch and it's hard to find good local food, but if you ask around and hug the side roads, the countryside and the rich barns and farmhouses, the quaint natives will take you away from the humdrum of reality.

Then you can take the Turnpike home and get back to civilization, quickly and vertically or maybe horizontally.

TEMPLE UNIVERSITY

Temple University is now celebrating its Diamond Jubilee and it just seems like yesterday when I was taken to hear the late great Dr. Russell Conwell deliver his famous "Acres of Diamonds" lecture. (It wasn't until I read it years later that I appreciated it.)

Dr. Conwell started Temple College in 1884 with the idea that you should teach anybody anything they wanted to learn, from ministry to embalming. He started with seven pupils and since then five hundred thousand have taken courses. The present enrollment is approximately thirty thousand and most of them are Philadelphians.

You would think with this remarkable achievement that Temple men would be as stuffy as the Ivy poison set, but they started modest and stay modest. Some of my best friends and family are T-men and they are outstanding Doctors, Lawyers, Judges, Artists and Head Shrinkers.

The international figure at Temple used to be Dr. Chevalier Jackson who invented the bronchoscope, which is something you stick down kids' throats when darling swallows an open safety pin. Dr. Jackson would close the pin and save it for the Temple collection of things kids enjoy munching. Dr. Jackson passed away some years after the invention of Dr. Spock (Yale '25). Spock has successfully ruined childhood by making mothers know all about everything in a paperback and not allowing kids to swallow anything except maybe the old man on weekends.

Temple has moved far afield from Russell Conwell's day. Now there are campuses all over town and there are sixteen separate schools and colleges. But old College Hall remains on Broad Street, a rusticated appendage to Baptist Temple. If you think Modern Architecture is difficult to explain away, this antique, crenelated, massive, domed, brutal stonework is even more puzzling. I guess they should preserve it for posterity and maybe even force a little ivy to grow (right out of the subway). It is a symbol of how hard our ancestors struggled to give us the fine sense of appreciation of education and the true values of attainment, strength and beauty, even though now in steel and plate glass, air conditioning and television. Next question. . . .

I was trying to figure out why suddenly I am so pro-Temple and I guess it is because I am probably one of the oldest living students I find. At the tender age of five my family thought I should be Jascha Heifetz, or even my Uncle Arthur, so they enrolled me in the Columbia College of Music on 15th at Columbia Avenue. That was an early Temple campus. My scratch sheet, or whatever you call those musical score books, shows that I lasted exactly three lessons and drew pictures instead of scoring "Through the Meadows Green I Flow."

That is why I am down here instead of onstage at the Academy of Moosic.

POLICE HEADQUARTERS

When you wish to gag on Philadelphia and its pious phony virtues, the greatest authority was a nobleman, Claude William Dukinfield (otherwise known as W. C. Fields), whose biography is a must on every shelf, along with a dry martini for after a hard day in town.

Mr. D. left Philadelphia at an early age and roamed the world trying to find a life better than in Philadelphia, and I think his only nod to us for superiority was that the jails here were better than anywhere in the world, and he seemed to have sampled a lot of them.

"When you get right down to it, there's nothing like Philadelphia," he would say, and his face would become animated as he recalled the gentility of the keepers, the thick bean soup and the scrubbed burlap rags.

I, who am an authority on nothing but a snooper into everything architectural, know little of the creature comforts of jails, although if I keep writing sooner or later my curiosity may be satisfied.

Once when I was a student, many, many years ago, I paid a visit to the Eastern Penitentiary to study its design, made internationally famous by Charles Dickens. My mentor was a psychology major who was doing his field work for his thesis on the "harsh treatment theme." He explained carefully to me that the three guys who had dug a tunnel right out into Callowhill Street were not trying to escape but were merely appealing to the civilised world for a fairer understanding of the prisoners' problem!

He introduced me to a lot of his subject matter and on the surface they all seemed as nice as my nephews, in fact nicer. When we left, my psychology major felt for his wallet, which was gone along with his scarf pin, pocket watch and chain and Phi Beta Kappa key. I think the only thing the boys left on him was his class ring which they probably didn't have time to saw off. Me, they did not frisk, probably sensing that an architectural student didn't have enough to make it worth while. Besides I tickle easy.

What this is all leading up to is that I have to draw that new glamorous Police Headquarters and I can't wait much longer for it to get finished. From the outside it looks like a good jail should, only modern, and it should scare the britches off anybody who has criminal intent because it would seem to be almost impregnable and certainly undefilable. I guess it is wonderful architecture and I who am not yet up on the bubble-gum school of design can only see in those curves a massive ad for "Maidenform Brassieres."

The big guffaw, esthetically speaking, (what with all this "form following function" and all that jazz) is that the place only looks jaily but aint no jail at all. It's nothing but a big blown-up office for cops and has maybe one stand-up room and a couple of polished cells just for quiet snoozing and showing off a rough guy to the press photographers.

Of course what is interesting also about the gem of planning is that it is located in what is and always was, as far as I can remember, the tenderloin of Philadelphia. Even today you shouldn't approach the section without a spray of flea powder and leave it with a complete prophylaxis and turkish bath with steam.

So any poor culprit who can loose his shackles and get across that Vine Street traffic alive can be in perfect heaven in a moment, lost to the cops and enveloped by soup kitchens, flophouses, missions, cheap saloons, barber schools, all night movies, and that most wonderful of all entertainments, the windows of the pawn shops and second hand dealers with acres of saxophones, binoculars, drafting instruments, ice skates, in fact everything no respectable bum would be caught with, but worth a night's sleep and a handout if you can snatch 'em and hock 'em.

STATE CAPITOL

Next Tuesday all the tumult and shouting will end and the nuisances will stop pestering you to vote for you-know-who.

I, who am not able to buy a job, limit my political activities to growling at my friends' wives, who should be home over a hot stove instead of honeying up to me for my measly vote.

The object of my affections will soon be raised to the mighty seat of Governor of Pennsylvania. But for that privilege he will have to live in Harrisburg for four years.

There, surrounded by some very fine examples of Architecture and Art, he will direct a lot of old hands, now passing as new brooms to sweep the place clean and bring some jobs back to Pennsylvania.

The Capitol building is a fine old upstanding bit of State Capitol architecture, based upon a Renaissance facade and capped by a beautiful dome which is almost but not St. Peter's in Rome.

On the very top is a figure, which every schoolboy knows represents "The Commonwealth" because he is holding up a garlanded mace.

I guess that I should quote here the famous words of William Penn:

"There may be room there for such a holy experiment. For the nations want a precedent. And my God will make it the seed of a nation. That an example may be set up to the nations. That we may do the thing that is truly wise and just."

These words of the founder are carved around the rotunda under the cornice, in case you wish the children to be inspired and crane their little necks.

Of course the entrance is flanked by George Gray Barnard's heroic symbolic spiritual sculpture.

There is a wonderful tile floor, full of Pennsylvania symbolism, animals and birds, the work of Henry Mercer of Doylestown. In the Senate chamber are the paintings of Edwin Austin Abbey and Violet Oakley. And so on and around are objects to inspire not only the highest white-vested authority but also the lowliest, coming hat in hand and contribution receipt in pocket.

Well, that's where the Governor presides and go shake his hand after New Year's day.

Around and about are other fine buildings and works of art worthy of your notice and it's a nice day's outing depending upon whom you may wish to consult.

MASONIC TEMPLE

If you hurry and stand with your back to Penn Center on 15th at the Parkway and look across you may gaze upon the devastation wrought by those brothers grim, the City Planning Commission. What used to be a fine open square with trees and a bandstand and a couple of heroic statues and plenty of benches for catching the last warmth of sunlight is now bulldozed in preparation for a new City Hall annex and enough underground garage space to satisfy the Philadelphia lawyer set and their ilk.

This not only ruins the square but also kills one of the finest architectural compositions, the graceful focal point of the Parkway. Around that square are the noble City Hall, the beautiful Masonic Temple, and a gem, the Arch St. M. E. Church.

When the new building is completed all gripes will, long since, have been silenced and the savage destruction of old trees will be shrugged off as progress and there we go looking like all other dull cities. But mostly the Masonic Temple won't ever again look right without some green near it. (And none of this fast line about new trees springing up overnight, what with twenty feet of subway before you can get a decent root.)

What I started to call your attention to before I cross my deadline is the Masonic Temple, designed in 1868 by James H. Windrim. He was a graduate of Girard College and I guess he didn't get any architectural training, except if you have been inside the college walls you may realize that what Mr. Windrim saw was all Greek Architecture, pure, simple and highly refined.

Greek architecture is hard enough to take when you are Socrates or Plato but on a growing boy its effect must have been depressing. The result is that Mr. Windrim didn't use a single Classic motif when he designed the Masonic Temple. At that time City Hall was just a gleam in some stone contractor's good eye.

Masonic Temple was supposed to be taller than anything and the view from the tower was visited by millions. Although Windrim's exterior is Norman in style he went eclectic wild on the interiors what with Gothic, Moorish and Egyptian halls, an Italian Renaissance library, a Corinthian staircase and a lot of other details which look well as a background for the gorgeous plumes and braid of the well-dressed Mason.

Well, Masonic Temple and its high tower were dedicated in September 1873. In July 1874 the cornerstone of City Hall was laid and that zillion-foot tower ruined everything in the tower competition. Also in July 1874 Charley Ross was kidnaped, but at that time I was only a gleam in my grandmother's eye . . . but what's that got to do with Masonic Temple?

OLDE BARBER SHOPPE

When I think that I have now had over a thousand haircuts by talkative barbers, you would expect that I would be able to find an old-fashioned barber shop. But it took the great help of Mr. Charles T. Bryan of the Atwater Kent Museum (where you may find out anything which I don't know about Philadelphia) to locate Loscalzo's on South 2nd Street which is a sanitary museum piece.

Now barbershops have gone hygienic and dull with maybe an electric barber pole and certainly no copy of the Police Gazette, no polished brass spittoons and positively no individual cups, except for decoration.

Most men have a favorite barber and a comfortable hour every couple of weeks, but I just move around mostly.

There isn't much personality or charm about modern barber shops. They are the last outpost of man, except on Saturday when Mom takes the kids in for haircuts which is a waste of an expert tonsorialist's time. Also, women in a barbershop make everybody and the manicurist uncomfortable and self-conscious.

Thinking of barbers reminds me of the time I was working on the design of the First World War American Battle Monument at Bony-Bellicourt in France and how a barber finished my story for me.

The design was a pair of square piers supporting an entablature, and General Foch said it looked like a gibbet. This made the architect, Paul Cret, sore and he redesigned it as a flat slab decorated with a battle map of the area.

But the design really should have been a gibbet because in that battle the American troops met the worst disaster of the war. The Twenty-Seventh and Thirtieth Divisions had been sent into the lines there for the first time and the big idea was to pierce the Hindenburg Line.

We were flanked by the French and the Australians and the order was to blast through the German line and advance a couple of kilometers and stop and dig in. The attack came off on schedule and the Germans dropped back. But somebody had forgotten that the Bony-Bellicourt sector was on top of the subterranean St. Quentin canal tunnel which the Germans had floored over and in that tunnel was the second German line. So that as the first wave of Americans came over, the Germans fell back, then the second line came up out of the tunnel and boxed and massacred us.

Well, after the war I was trying to piece together the points of advance of our troops so I could draw a fairly accurate map and have it carved on the memorial. We sent letters to men in both Divisions and pinpointed the locations and they had wandered all over the place in all directions.

For several years I kept asking everybody where he had been on the night of September 27, 1918, and one day I was getting a tony haircut in the Bellevue. The barber was gassing about the war and I asked him. He was at Bony all right. He was with the Twenty-Seventh and was the general's barber.

On the night before the attack the general called him and said to him, "I will be at a place called Guillemont farm," and he showed him on the map. The general said, "Tony, you stay the hell back here and in the morning come over to the farmhouse and shave me."

The barber stayed back and went over in the morning, complete with G.I. razors, soap and towels and tonic, but found not his general. Three days and six kilometers over that way, he found him.

"Mr. Bendiner," said the barber, "I want to tell you something. Did that general need a shave!"

THE BULLETIN
BUILDING

Ever since I started this thankless task of educating an appreciative public in the values and nuances of fine and delicate achievements in Architecture around this area, I have been given the hotfoot by some of what might be called my friends for not taking a pass at The Bulletin Building.

But The Bulletin Building has already been praised in highfalutin' prose by no less a character than Dr. Lewis Mumford, and he likes everything including the spacing of the silver lettering on the main facade and also the flagpole and surrounding granite cobble-stones.

The Bulletin Building is a good example of what we get rammed down us as beautiful, beautiful, and I guess it's beautiful and not just the bare bones of a beauty. What I mean

is that you have to stand back and realize that here is a symphony in fine proportion with just the most delicate balance held by silver columns, and the brick wall charmingly accented with perfectly spaced lettering which will slowly make you realize that you are gazing ecstatically at the workshop of the greatest newspaper in Philadelphia. And the only other break in the calm serenity of the facade is a well proportioned electric sign which slowly wafts golden letters across the face informing you capsulely of the time and the weather and a wisp of the great news which will be yours if you only get *The Evening Bulletin*.

But beyond this gay mask lies the interesting world of freight cars, rolls of paper from the great forest, and the maze of machinery

and presses. And above, the workers are punching away at their typewriters with butterfly fingers and gossamer copy paper, working with beaverish fury to meet every deadline, check and double check every comma, read and reread every stick of their efforts to bring you the best in news. It all must be seen to be appreciated and there are guided tours where you may watch Editor Bergman scissoring away.

But Beauty is in the eye of the beholder and I am now down to trifocals, so I am not a fair judge. To get to my Editor and meet a deadline I have to go to the brain center of the newspaper business, the editorial department. This is situated as far away from the main entrance as the architects could conceive. You have to go down a long entrance

corridor, up three flights on a slow escalator, down a long dreary hall, and way out there in West Philadelphia is where all that wonderful *Sunday Bulletin Magazine* is written. By the time you get the copy down you are footsore, weary and exhausted and hardly in shape to enjoy the fine proportions and delicate coloring, which I am sure are there if you took the time to notice them.

The Bulletin Building was designed by George Howe who designed PSFS, the outstanding building in Philadelphia and most of the United States, and his partner Robert Montgomery Brown, a handsome lad and a capable one who looks well in a short caracul coat and a pearl gray derby.

I guess I am just not for this era of progress because I was weaned in the newspaper business in the art department of the old Public Ledger at 5th and Chestnut Streets, and my job as copy boy was to keep the wine cooled in the water cooler and paste up copy. The room was on the third floor of a ratty firetrap and the art department gentlemen were all hefty eaters, drinkers and cigar smokers, who seemed to work right through days and nights, Sundays and holidays, without the need of sleep or change in laundry.

It was all rugged and good-old-daysey and just like the newspaper boys you see in the movies, and hardly the place to allow a sensitive juvenile just ready for Art school, smocks, daisy painting and a live model in one hand and a copy of Royal Cortissoz in the other.

Well, here am poor old I, fifty years later, expected to be appreciative and joyous about a sanitary structure which coddles a lot of nine to five air-cooled journalists, with time and a half for over time and none of your half pints stashed in a roachy wooden locker.

It's all much better and I know it, but it comes hard to me who now can't stay up half the night and drink my share without double migraines, acid indigestion, crawlies and all those things you have to take for doing what used to come naturally.

THE GIRARD TRUST
BUILDING

Long ago when people lived in the city there was a saloon on every corner and some joyful architecture. But Prohibition changed all those wicked thoughts. Now there is a bank on every corner waiting to be merged or embezzled.

The Great White Buddha of them all sits on the northwest corner of Broad and Chestnut Streets. It looks fat and lovely and Classical—snooty even though it is towered over and shadowed by many-storied skyscrapers.

The Girard Trust Co., or whatever its latest merger name, was designed by Stanford White, who made the sketches and then went over to Madison Square Garden for a jeroboam of champagne and got shot by Harry K. Thaw. It was all very sad.

McKim, Meade and White were the great architects of the Classic period in American architecture, and following Mr. White's demise, Classic declined in favor of Frank Lloyd Wright, if you think *that* was an improvement.

If you never were in Rome, Italy, and were taught never to correct your elders, you are supposed to believe that the building is an exact copy of the Pantheon in Rome. Well, this much is to be said: it has a portico (Ionic instead of Corinthian), a pediment, a dome (marble instead of concrete) and an oculus (covered instead of open.) Inside, the place is full of bankers (instead of tourists.)

From there on you can study the post cards for our weekly course in Architecture.

Around on the Chestnut Street facade you can see where the bank ran out of money, for the cymatium is only carved with acanthus leaves for a couple of feet, and the rest of the cornice left bare and unadorned.

Everybody wants to tear down City Hall, but nobody could even get a letter published daring to suggest that they tear down the G. T. Building. Once it was suggested that it be taken down stone by stone and rebuilt on top of a sixty-story office building but nothing came of it.

I used to think that you had to have a letter of introduction from a member of the Philadelphia Club before you could deposit there, but a couple of years ago my cousin Artie came out fondling a fresh green pile of payroll money and he was promptly shanghaied and relieved of his wealth by a zealous and vigilant holdup man who, it turned out, was a stranger in town from New York.

I guess the most important asset the Girard Trust has, for me, is the chestnut man who stands right on the corner of Broad and CHESTNUT Streets and sells hot chestnuts, which are very good and keep your hands warm, twenty-five cents a package.

THE HEAD HOUSE

The Head House stands at the head of a wreck known as the Second Street Market which was the oldest market in the United States and was going strong until a couple of years ago when Philadelphia got planned.

To us, Christmas was for children, and the big treat was to be taken to the wonderful 2nd Street Market. The place was an enclosed, unventilated, unheated, unkempt, unsanitary building one story high and a block long. Inside, at Christmas, the whole place was ablaze with colored lights, loaded with greens and tinsel and stocked with food which you didn't see around all the rest of the year. On most family market days, we were in school, but at the holiday season we were allowed to go and even spend a dime.

You went to market not only to buy things but also to smell them and squeeze them, weigh them in your hand and poke at the livestock to see if it was corn-filled. You knew everybody and could spot a salesman who was weighing his thumb in with your hamburger order.

And there was a wonderful symphony of sounds and a variety of smells of humans and animals, fish and fowl, vegetables, cheese and soggy floor sawdust.

The outer perimeter was lined with trees and wreaths and mistletoe, and big cardboard boxes of bells and ornaments and stands of grave decorations in high color. The streets were crowded with huckster trucks and steaming horses and the air was filled with the smell of greens burning in the braziers. You lined your pockets with hot chestnuts to keep your hands from freezing, or you sucked endlessly on hard candy figures of animals or Santa Claus.

Well, it's all gone now and nothing remains but the Head House and the abandoned market. The Head House, which was the meeting place for the area in the Eighteenth Century, is all restored and looks like a nice, dead, inhuman, don't-touch museum. Around and about is the wreckage of progress just awaitin' for Uncle Sam to fix it up and phony Colonial the area to show Aunt Hattie and the cousins from Tacoma.

120

LIT BROTHERS

You wouldn't believe it except that I told you, but this corner of Lit Brothers is one of the earliest and also the last remaining examples of an advance in Architecture, the pre-cast iron facade.

It retained the classic arched opening and was made to look like stone by Collins and Autenrieth, but it's all iron and its value was that you didn't have to fireproof the inside. But I don't want to get into that now.

More important to me is a sign which still appears on Lit Brothers front which says "Hats trimmed free of charge."

Which I can hang a story upon, because once in Paris we went to a chapellerie or ladies' hat store. By the time we got charmed into three hats I had figured enough French to ask for a receipt and I told the gentleman I was from Philadelphie, Pennsylvanie. The proprietor's eyes lit up like he was really pleased and he said, "Bon, bon, ah, Philadelphie. Is the place across from Camden, New Jersey, no?"

"Oui," said I, "except we used to think it was the other way 'round, but how do you know about Camden, New Jersey?"

"Well," he said, "during the Great War there is American battery stationed with anti-aircraft in the Place St. Michel and one night my wife she is giving birth to the baby and so I go to the sergeant and ask permission to cross the Seine for getting the Docteur.

"Well, the sergeant wanted to know what's the need for a Docteur, so I told him, and he said when the baby is born let us know and we will all having a drink.

"So, my son he is born and the sergeant and the gun crew come in and we all have a drink all around and the sergeant says the crew is adopting the boy and will send him to Medical School.

"Now he is almost going to school and every year I am getting the money from the battery for educating my son and he is adopted by the battery from Camden, New Jersey, in the United States."

Except I forgot to ask him the number of the battery so I could give them a credit line right here, now.

122

VALLEY GREEN

Some of the best people I know never get enough of snow. I believe that the blizzard of 1888 was sufficient; my poor mother had to climb out the second-story window and walk through the drifts to work at Hirsh and Bros. umbrella factory, and we heard about it for some generations now.

But snow is something not only to shovel but enjoy, particularly if you wish you had been born a hundred years ago when everything was romantic, if cold and uncomfortable.

To get really into the spirit of the thing you should heigh-ho and away you go to Valley Green where you may still to this day hire a sleigh and a steaming, spirited bay complete with jingle bells, moth-eaten buffalo robes and water-logged foot warmers. It's Fairmount Park, which doesn't recognize alcohol as the milk of middle age so you have to carry your own like Prohibition.

Valley Green is situated over this way from Mom Rinker's Rock. Mom Rinker was a kindly old spy who worked for General Washington. She sat on the rock knitting day after day and watching the British troops go by. They just thought she was a nice old lady but really she was counting something like "Knit one, purl two and there go the 17th Grenadier Guards," and passing on the information to the Colonials hiding in the bushes.

Valley Green has a quaint history all its own. It has been there, I think, since somewhere around 1681, but George Washington never slept there. He was encamped at Barren Hill but for the first time stayed out in the cold with his men. Legend has it that Washington and Lafayette stopped at Valley Green for dinner, but I guess they couldn't get a port or a Madeira or even a cool spot of Liebfraumilch with their chicken, so they left.

That proves how long ago the Fairmount Park Commission has owned the place.

Anyhow you may go now and dine sumptuously and dryly at Valley Green, and pick a nice cold and frosty evening with the air charged with something and a million stars and peace and quiet and all blissy and you can imagine what it must have been like to have been a colonist, or an Indian.

PHILADELPHIA ART ALLIANCE

Say something nice, says the Boss. So now that The Art Alliance has gone pretty liberal for a Philadelphia Club, let us consider it, and also the architecture in which it is housed.

About forty years ago it used to be real Philadelphia stuffy and Bohemian for Walnut Street with a long dining table, candlelight, polished brass and a sort of warm sepia air with a bit of gamboge once in a while for brilliance. Clara Mason was teaching little Miss Dorothy Kohl to be an executive secretary and run the joint and not get it jumping beyond the tea and crumpets and hot milk stage.

In 1926 The Art Alliance moved to its present home at Rittenhouse Square and Eighteenth. From then on it has been onwards and upwards with the Arts as the main motif, and an open house to the Public Art Gallery run by the Club. If you can do any kind of Art up to Tattooing and can pass those Committees you can become a member for less money than a mere appreciator who pays more for sitting around and listening to the rare air of Art Talk.

I love The Philadelphia Art Alliance with a true, undying, forty-five-year membership love, and as long as Archie stays behind the bar and the boys and girls who run the place keep pleasant and nurse the old folks along, Art will hold its head high in Philadelphia.

The building is something else again. It is likely to be preserved and is a fine example of a town house of the elegant era before taxes and nobody wanting to do housework and live on the fourth floor. Despite its austere, Renaissancy, "keep out" exterior, The Art Alliance is really a warm, open to the public, free exhibition of all kinds of Art, from everywhere, and subject to change to keep it alive and interesting. Also there are lectures and other fringe benefits.

You and your children and grandchildren should go often. Outside of Philadelphia the Art Alliance is thought of as highly as The Orchestra and our one or two other aesthetic assets. The only portion reserved for the members is the restaurant and bar.

One more thing and then you can get your Sunday nap. The building was designed by that great Philadelphia architect, Frank Miles Day, in 1906 for the Wetherills. The founder of The Art Alliance was a Wetherill, Mrs. Yorke Stevenson. The Art Alliance bought the Wetherill residence in 1926, and it is now a sort of memorial to the founder and right there in her childhood home.

FLEISHER ART
MEMORIAL

Today when everybody's Mom is a painter and can spot a fake Renoir faster than you can say John Canaday, I guess it is corny to still think the Graphic Sketch Club is a worthy Art Institution, but it sure is.

I am surprised to find that three thousand boys and girls and more mature artists still go down there and enjoy just plain drawing and painting without feeling that they are awful special and rare talents.

Like almost everybody who wore a smock a couple of generations ago, I spent a part of my night life down in Little Italy learning to drink red wine, twirl spaghetti and draw at the Graphic Sketch Club.

This is a gift to Philadelphia by Samuel S. Fleisher, a yarn manufacturer with no art ability or training. He loved underprivileged slum people and believed that if you exposed kids to Beauty they would grow up to be real charming instead of rat-tatting around scaring the neighbors.

With this lofty purpose in mind Mr. Fleisher bought the building of the St. Martin's College of the Church of the Evangelists in 1916, and set it up as a free four-story Art School, filled with lifelike portraits and other paintings plus realistic sculpture, ceramics, porcelains, ivory carvings, brasses, bronzes, and early Etruscan pottery and jewelry—the kind of art you don't see much of nowadays any more.

The place was open to everybody day and night. There were no guards and nothing was locked but curiously, nobody stole anything. The school and galleries were a sort of Holy Experiment which worked.

Right alongside the school was the abandoned Church of the Evangelists. In 1922 Mr. Fleisher acquired that and connected it to the school. He called it The Sanctuary and declared it open to all faiths and restored it and added to its former glory.

The Sanctuary was the brainchild of the Rev. Dr. Henry Robert Percival who in 1880 had been keen on reproducing an Italian Basilica type of church in Philadelphia. It was to have "the relative proportions of the Basilica of Pisa, the square pillars of St. Mark's and the sanctuary square as in the Cathedral of Orvieto." The exterior is of brick with a portico supported by columns resting upon the backs of a pair of uncarved lions like the Cathedral at Verona, if I remember the slide. And it is easier to visit than going all the way to Italy to see the same things only larger.

Then Fleisher left the Club and the Sanctuary, and enough money to keep them going, to the city—no "museum art," just a nice simple, quiet, unpretentious Art School.

Of course, Committees can't leave anything sweet alone, so now that it is an adjunct of the Museum it is a sort of "Luxembourg to the Louvre" they tell me, which sounds good if you ain't never seen the Louvre or the Luxembourg.

And of course, all the "art" stuff which I was raised on has been cleared out and the place is painted, scrubbed and full of authenticated *Art* objects, fine religious paintings, ecclesiastical sculpture and a mile of ikons.

So if you are in the neighborhood of Eighth and Catharine buying an eel and wish to rest your tired feet you may enjoy a quiet hour in the peace of the Sanctuary and look around at the work of old Philadelphia artists like Violet Oakley, Nicola D'Ascenzo, Samuel Yellin, Mary Alice Nielson, Robert Henri and many, many others who studied at Graphic.

MR. GRAFF'S MEMORIAL

On July 4, 1786, olde style, Benjamin Henry Latrobe was walking absentmindedly down Sixth Street toward the market when he almost tripped over young Frederick Graff (1777-1847). Thus began a beautiful friendship and hence the Philadelphia Water Works, the surrounding gardens and eventually Fairmount Park.

The water works group sits along the Schuylkill, now glowered over by the Art Museum. It is a beautiful crumble and until recently had in its damp, dank, unkempt interior the disgraceful Aquarium.

Well the fish are gone South and I guess now we will be in for a move to ax the buildings because they probably stand in the way of Progress.

Mr. Latrobe and Mr. Graff designed and built the whole water works system which brought Schuylkill water to the thirsty Philadelphians. You would hardly think that anybody who drank the stuff would put up money for a memorial, but there in his garden sits Mr. Graff in a perpendicular Gothic monument with a touch of Dowling in the foliations.

Mr. Isaac Levy of the Fairmount Park Commission thinks the Museum lacks initiative. They bought a Walt Kuhn. Mr. Levy likes *Custer's Last Stand.*

Now, I think the Fairmount Park Commission could show some initiative by restoring the Water Works and making it into a gay Vienna beer garden complete with singing waiters, gypsy orchestra and enough room in the pergola to swing a czardas or a wild cancan. There is enough space around the museum at the terrace level to house a couple of thousand cars.

Well, you know how it is, what with a couple of beers and a good slow Blue Danube waltz and heigh ho, even Mr. Levy might throw away four bits and go into the Museum, just to cool off, and maybe cast a side glance at St. Gaudens' *Diana* or try and figure Titian's *Europa and the Bull,* and gradually move onward and upward to Schamberg's abstraction made of plumbing fixtures.

With all that money rolling in, the City could locate *Custer's Last Stand* and buy it for the Museum.

I, too, wouldn't mind seeing it again and it would be a great relief as a chaser to Rico LeBrun, Motherwell and Jackson Pollock, which you can see in any other Museum.

THE PHILADELPHIA
SKATING CLUB AND
HUMANE SOCIETY

There used to be ice skating on the Schuyl-kill, and even on the Delaware, at least once, long enough to get a picture painted.

In the early days of the countrie, "Phila-delphians were the best and most elegant skaters in the world." Benjamin West the painter wowed the English on the Serpentine by cutting the "Philadelphia salute." General Cadwalader, Theodore Massey the biscuit maker, and a "black skater who outstripped the wind" have gone down in my history book.

As you might guess, all this fun couldn't just go along in Philadephia without forming a club, so The Skater's Club started and later merged with the Humane Society, and to this very day we have "The Philadelphia Skating Club and Humane Society."

The original purpose was to instruct and improve the art of skating and the efficient use of proper apparatus to rescue persons breaking through the ice. The members did a lot of rescuing until 1860, when they just set-tled down to plain and fancy skating. That's

when the Clubhouse was built on the banks of the Schuylkill above the dam at Fairmount. Now it's a part of Boathouse row and rented out to a Girl's Rowing Club.

The Skating Club still functions at a swish big heated rink out in Ardmore. It has over six hundred members and five hundred kids all going like mad from November to May, come winter's icy blasts or balmy approaches to spring. You can't very well fall through the ice and get rescued because the artificial glaze is only about four inches thick above a con-crete floor, but the old ropes and belts and lifesaving apparatus are around the walls, just in case of. . . .

And if you are real good and get invited on Saturday afternoon, you may have a cheering cup and dance and maybe cut "The Philadel-phia Salute" just for old times sake.

I, who once fell on the ice and broke my hand and a syllabub glass brimful of dry mar-tini, stay away from such dangerous areas as rinks, ponds, and lakes, but I seem to be in the vast minority.

THE ATHENAEUM

I guess that this is about the last private Library in Philadelphia which has so far not been swallowed by Big Daddy on the Parkway.

It was founded as a reference library where you might find books which you can't find in other libraries. It still sticks to its original purpose.

To become a member you have to wait for another old Philadelphian to die and have his family relinquish the share, so it's available to some other old Philadelphian. That's a long wait, but worthwhile if you are going back where you came from—Society Hill. The Library is on Washington Square, and the building was designed by Charles Notman, and is still the best architectural thing around.

If you wish to see a historical monument which has not changed since it was built in 1847, complete with the original chandeliers, furniture, chess room, barometer, pictures and members, just pop in any time and leave your calling card.

The building at various times has housed not only the Athenaeum, but also the American Institute of Architects, The Venezuelan and British Consulates, the Law Library and the Historical Society of Pennsylvania. Now the Maritime Museum is there.

The most awe-inspiring room is the Main Library on the second floor. It is as stuffy looking and quiet as Colonel Blimp's Boodles Club in London, except that the director and the girls who run the place are really alive and very pleasant. Looking from the much-too-tall windows to the garden there is a trellis which has, without question, the biggest gnarled wisteria vine planted by John Wistar, who looked up and said, "I name thee Wisteria," about which there have been arguments ever since.

I, a working newspaper man, am entitled by the Act of the Pennsylvania Legislature not to have to reveal the sources of my information. I would say that I was told all this Wistar story by my Grandmother on her knee, except both my Grandmothers spoke only pure Hungarian and pronounced the English W as V, so I am probably mistaken, as usual.

THE WALNUT STREET
THEATRE

I guess you could say, I mean I guess I could say, the most undistinguished-looking distinguished theatre surviving in the whole English-speaking world is here at 9th and Walnut Streets, Philadelphia 7, Pa.

It was built in 1806, and was originally a circus. Later it became a theatre and Thomas Jefferson and the Marquis de Lafayette slept right through *The Rivals* at the opening in 1812; except the Walnut was then known as the Olympia. Edwin Forrest played there and then the place reverted back to a circus and then back to a theatre and here we are.

At various times everybody who was "so much better than anybody you see nowadays" appeared there, like Edwin Forrest, Louisa Lane (Mrs. John Drew), Charlotte Cushman (who caught cold playing *Romeo*), Mrs. Jefferson, the grandmother of Joe Jefferson (*Rip Van Winkle*), Edmund Kean, and of course Junius Brutus Booth.

In 1920 the whole interior was replaced with a modern steel fireproof structure resembling the old place and George Arliss opened in *The Green Goddess*.

But probably the greatest eye-opener to Philadelphia was in April, 1930, on a cool spring evening, when that little Georgia peach Miss Miriam Hopkins came onstage as *Lysistrata*, the Greek girl who figured out the most awful way to end wars. She was dressed in a diaphanous Bonwit Teller nightie like you buy your wife at Christmas and only that covered a beautiful 18 year-old figure.

Since the play was by some old goat named Aristophanes and the sponsors were the snooty Furness family of University of Pennsylvania fame, it hardly seemed appropriate to call in the gendarmes and stop Art. I guess it would be mild compared to the movies today, but it was hot stuff for 1930, even though it has been in print since about 400 B.C.

Anyhow, it was a turkey nobody but the Furnesses would have bought. Wonder what ever happened to Miss Hopkins? She was a lovely, and opposite fat old Sydney Greenstreet, of all people. Must read *Lysistrata* some day. I bet it's real corn.

137

PENNSYLVANIA
HOSPITAL

A psychiatrist once said to me, "The trouble with you is that you don't have any inhibitions."

But I have a couple: Religion and Hospitals. They both scare me and I stay clear of them as long as possible, but my luck can't hold forever.

So, if I have any choice, I prefer one of those old Colonial rooms at Pennsylvania Hospital. Not that it is any more modern, sanitary, or has a better staff than any of the hundred other hospitals. But I guess I would be more comfortable, even under the worst physical circumstances, if I were bedded in a room with a wooden floor, painted mouldings, maybe even a carved cornice, and perhaps a corny picture on the wall.

But I guess I'll wind up in a hygienic, dustproof, cinderblock cubbyhole, complete with radio, television, electric eyes and every new mechanical gadget designed to get you up and out two days after you have just gotten settled and about to enjoy the nurses.

The Pennsylvania Hospital, Eighth and Spruce, cornerstone laid 8 A.M., May 28, 1755; the above wing by David Evans 1794; in the garden a lead figure of William Penn. Inside *Christ Healing the Sick in the Temple*, a painting by Benjamin West, a couple of Sully landscapes, a handsome double staircase, a Rittenhouse orrery (planetarium to you), a working fire engine (1763), a wine cooler (2 shillings extra), a wonderful library and its wonderful librarian, Miss Eastburn. And a fine collection of memorabilia.

Where else can you see all these things for free, even if you are wheeling around the place looking pale, wan and dressed in pajamas and a dressing gown and carpet slippers like you would never be caught dead in at home.

Across the street is Lying-In, except you can't call it Lying-In any more because they stash men there. Anyhow, crowning that building is a cupola and on that a weather vane of a stork carrying a baby in an unsanitary flannel diaper. A touch of gayety, what . . . ?

138

P.S.F.S. BUILDING

One of the prize goofy theories of the city planner is that if you put a fine building in a dreary location, then everybody and his brother will immediately pitch in and make the surroundings just as beautiful as the gem your architect has erected. I don't know why I stick my neck out to point this up, but here I go again.

The greatest achievement here in Architecture and beautiful in pure spatial formalism and a couple of other "je ne sais quoi" isms is the P. S. F. S. Building at 12th and Market Streets. It has been there thirty years now which would seem long enough to influence a neighborhood, but it didn't.

When the big know-it-alls pick out the Hundred Best Buildings in the whole United States, Philadelphia gets one—P. S. F. S. The Society of Architectural Historians thinks it's fine enough to devote a whole volume to its merits, and it has long been recognized as an achievement in Modern Architecture which has stood the critical blah blah for lo these many years.

Of course it has a great architectural short-coming—that first floor. You would think that a fat rich bank with one hundred and fifty stories of rented office space and vaults bulging with moola would not have to rent out the first floor to a ready-to-wear dress shop, but there it is and very successful. Try and find the entrance to the office building which is stuck up a side street, or if you wish to deposit a measly few thousand sawbucks you must take a solid silver escalator to the second floor.

Well, there are two thousand other banks, maybe not as pretty where you may deposit your money right off the street, if you are in that much of a hurry.

The building is simply beautiful in all lights. The Architects were George Howe and William Lescaze and the arguments about who designed it are still punchy except that Lescaze is alive, so he wins. It must be seen to be appreciated, especially the Main Banking Room which is so discreet and soundproof you can't hear a dime drop; and the Board Room which is lined solid with gold-framed ancestors and has a nice view.

140

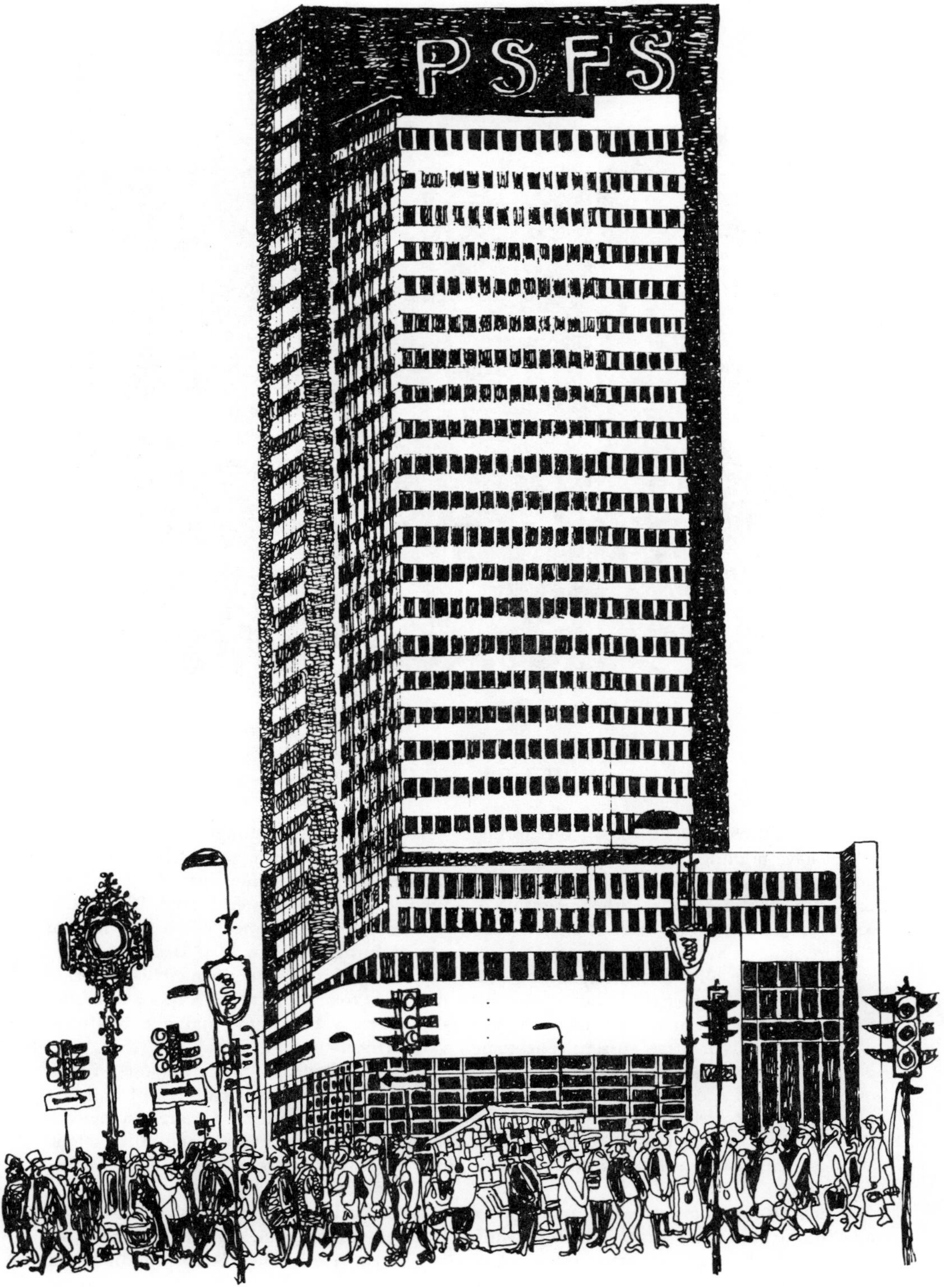
PSFS

DOGWOOD TIME AT
VALLEY FORGE

Oh the flowers that bloom in the Spring, tra-la, have nothing to do with the case; I've got to take under my wing, tra-la, a most unattractive old thing, tra-la, with a caricature of a face, tra-la, with a caricature of a face," sang Gilbert or was it Sullivan?

What brought all that on is blooming dogwood trees which upset everybody about this time and wreck a whole weekend for otherwise normal stay-at-home citizens. For come dogwood blossoms at Valley Forge, every car owner must up and away to see this annual phenomenon of sheer delight, loveliness and the boundless exuberance of Mother Nature at the vernal season, or let us call it Primavera for short.

If there is one thing which I cannot bring myself to, it is to make a two-column drawing of a dogwood blossom, so you get a drawing of Washington's Hdqs. at Valley Forge, suitable for framing. (Send twenty dollars in a self-addressed stamped envelope for a copy).

I used to like Washington's Headquarters at Valley Forge which should be really seen on a cold snowy evening just like 1778. But now that I am educated I read. That's bad because I find that the "house Washington rented furnished from Mrs. Deborah Hewes has no sophistication; is merely a Letitia house in stone; reflects old ways of building; the interiors are simple and not at all advanced for their day . . ."

I thought Pennsylvania farmhouses of variegated stone were wonderful. Now I find that "the textural beauties of rough stonework seem a perverse affectation, the villages look like so many clusters of jails and the public buildings like the Bastille."

Well, under those circumstances, I guess General Washington who had impeccable taste must have loathed the surroundings and probably preferred to sleep in one of those charming unheated log cabins.

FLOWER MART

Everything is late this spring, except maybe the date the income tax returns are due. But comes May and all the dear dears of the Hospital Ladies Aid Societies come in and take over Rittenhouse Square with little booths and potted plants and expensive hot dogs and high-pitched greetings and overdressed outdoorsy goodness for sweet charity's sake.

By this late date I should be used to seeing a lot of my friends passing as Marie Antoinette's scullery maids, or lower, but somehow the early bronze Chestnut Hill or is it Wayne veneer shows through and ruins everything.

Trouble with Philadelphia women is that they are much too straight and narrow for peasant stuff like birds, trees, flowers and mulching around in tight pants and big hats. Better they should relax and clip coupons and introduce stuffy luncheon speakers, or write books about Bostonians.

However, what I think about the inhabitants should not influence you. Please go to Rittenhouse Square, buy a couple of potted geraniums, two small phlox and a spray of iris, take a chance on a pony which you would not know what to do with if you won it and hope and pray you get some blueblooded doll as a Gray Lady or a nurses aid to take your blood or hand you a magazine if you ever get laid up at Bryn Mawr or Chestnut Hill instead of Philadelphia General or Einstein Southern, which are just as true but maybe not quite as blue.

Myself, on that day I always sit under Bayre's lovely lion and scare kids, stick pins in the balloons, throw rocks at the for-hire ponies, get in the way of the tintype photographer, and feed the don't-feed-the-pigeons and squirrels.

SCHUYLKILL
EXPRESSWAY

It's a shame about the Expressway. It should be a pleasant way to see some of the most interesting and beautiful views of Philadelphia, but it is mainly a noisy nightmare, a nervously blurred, jumpy, old-fashioned movie. I wish there was some way to slow it down, but I know it is impossible.

I find the best way to ride the Expressway is to scratch two rabbits' feet, pat my lucky moonstone, count my Arab fidget beads, count ten, spit into the wind, say my private Devil-Worshipper's prayer, and slip into the traffic stream.

I try and remember everything which I have read and heard from the adjoining seat in 45 years of fairly safe driving: "Keep in your lane and don't straddle the white line. Stay seventy-five feet behind the maniac in front. Turn off the radio. Watch the blond in the midget cutting into my fender. Push off

the left turn signal. Oops, watch the truck birdie, duck your head and be ready to ditch as the trailer tilts over the guard rail. Hold your hats as she levels off. Now head into the left lane and speed her up. No! The cop in the Red Car is looking into your rear mirror."

Now you're past the mob and can breathe until they start mowing you down on all sides. Make up your mind—will you turn off toward North Philly, or cut into the slot and go down the East River Drive? It's clogged.

Maybe the entrance to West River is clear, but that guy sitting on your rear fender will kill you. So it's straight through. You should take a right at 30th Street, but you're boxed by trucks and trailers—so now for Center City. There goes 15th, 12th, Holy Mackerel, next chance off is the Bridge and Camden. Maybe it would be better to stay off the Expressway or let your wife drive.

ELFRETH'S ALLEY

I better say something sweet about Elfreth's Alley or I'll be ridden out of town on a hall-marked log. For Elfreth's Alley is about the last of the small streets near the river, and is kept alive and restored by a doughty band of deep city lovers, who really live there all year around and only let tourists gawk in the parlors once a year (which was yesterday). But you may see enough on the outside to satisfy curiosity. Insides are a lot like the highly restored Betsy Ross house around the corner.

The street, alley and courts are what Philadelphia looked like before we got planned. Except all that's left in Elfreth's Alley is now fancy-pantsied up; and behind the theatrical fronts there's none of this living by fireplace alone and drawing your water from the corner well. No, sir, it's all oil heat and air conditioning and all the other conveniences, well worked into the old inconveniences.

However, it's your last chance before the ax of Progress to get into arguments about whether the bricks are ballast brought from England, or really Early American brought by canoe from Burlington, New Jersey. The architecture has the character of an English village (except small paned double-hung windows instead of casements), paneled shutters and slat shutters, uncarved cornices and wood dormers, paneled front doors with brass knockers.

The cellarways are covered with a wood door, and a quaint foot scraper at each marble step. But no mud in the street, no horses, dogs, birds, trees, hawkers with street cries, knife grinders, glass cutters or Colonial dames scratching the flea bites. My, oh my, it must have been real comfy and cosy with everybody loving each other cometh cold of Winter or warmth of Summer.

Far as I can find out almost everybody real important lived hard-by or near the alley but mostly the neighbors were simple butcher, baker, candlestickmaker, boulter and smithy gentlefolk.

Someone once dropped a baby into the window of Mr. Sparhawks' home and it was raised by the family Donaldson. Wonder what's become of "Sally in our Alley"? I used to know a Sally Donaldson but she came from McKeesport.

But don't be snooty, a lot of nice families lived in Elfreth's Alley: Adam Clampffer, William Will, Israel Cassel, William Maugridge, Thomas Potts, Moses Mordecai, Jacob I. Cohen, Daniel Haley and many others. How's that for names-dropping?

GERMANTOWN
ACADEMY

School Days, school days, dear old golden rule days, taught to the tune of a hickory stick, OUCH!

Summer is icumen, loud cry the released educated little ones. So let us bow toward the oldest school in the United States and the Colonies in almost continuous use since the wholesome idea was discussed over a mug of mulled ale and wienerwurst at Daniell Mackinet's tavern on the cold evening of December 6, 1759.

Opened 1762, as the Union School of Germantown, now known as Germantown Academy, with sixty students "birched" in the German department by Hilarius Becker, and seventy "tanned" in the English department by "the stern Master David James Dove." The Founding Fathers were English, German, Swedish and Dutch and in their religious beliefs Quaker, German Reformed, Mennonite, Lutheran, Dunker and Separatist.

In genuine union and tolerance they agreed that "the said schoolhouse should be free to all persons of what denomination soever and wheresoever residing, to send their children thereto, without regard to name or sect of people, provided they be subject to the proper and necessary regulations of the master and trustees."

The building still functions as an upper school; the main body has moved to Fort Washington. The beautiful building still has the belfry with the weathervane carrying the "crown of England" and the old school bell still tolls the opening of the school day and if they win a game.

Washington lived there during the yellow fever epidemic and so did a couple of banks, The Pennsylvania and The Bank of North America.

Germantown Academy is not to be confused with Germantown Friends, except for a moment after scrimmage with the ball on the one-yard line and a lot of gentlefolk having the spirit move them at the same time on both sides of the field.

Myself, I am a kindergarten to college, Philadelphia Public School boy, so nobody would ask me how to solve these front page problems, but maybe it would have been better if my teachers had let me have a couple—just for remembrance.

At least I would have known how to spell, punctuate and add sums instead of leaving it all to a Germantown Friends School graduate to correct.

THE SCHUYLKILL NAVY

I always thought that Betsy Ross made the first flag for the Schuylkill Navy, but actually it was for the Pennsylvania Navy. The Schuylkill Navy (1858) is a fairly old Philadelphia institution and is well known wherever an oar is pulled or a toast is heisted.

It is a fine body of about a thousand men who spend their spare time rowing backwards on the Schuylkill in paper-thin boats, about an eighth of an inch thick and delicate. They share the honors of most of the twelve boat houses in Fairmount Park (one is occupied by the Girls Rowing Club—not members of the Navy) and they row in all weather except when there is a thin coat of ice on the water, which wrecks them.

The sport is cosmopolitan. Everybody rows and is healthy. Nobody has ever died while rowing, and a gentleman of over seventy-five has logged more than 26,000 miles without seeing where he was going.

Everybody keeps a record of his mileage and there are prizes, cups, pennants and testimonials lining the walls of the club houses, which are filled with shells of all sizes.

So hail to the Fourth of July and the Schuylkill Navy Regatta which is as famous as firecrackers and not as dangerous. And a salute to Bachelors, College, Crescent, Fairmount, Malta, Penn Athletic, Undine, University and Vesper. And any others who row the three-mile stretch from East Falls Bridge to Boat House Row and pull over just before going over the Fairmount Dam.

The "Navy" has produced a number of Diamond Sculls, Olympics and other champs such as Jack Kelly Senior and Jack Kelly Junior, Joe Burke, James Barker, Paul Costello and Charles MacIlvaine. Don't hit me with a coxswain if I miss a couple but a bow to Jim Juvenal, Miller, Myers and Gilmore and many others.

But I suppose the most famous immortalized oarsmen who ever wore a colorful red head handkerchief were painted by the now-acclaimed Thomas Eakins. I think they were Max Schmidt in a single shell and the Biglen Brothers in a "double."

You don't have to row to appreciate it. You may line the banks of the river or gawk sideways out of your moving car and enjoy somebody else working. I did pull an oar once in a row-boat in Willow Grove Park. That's how I know about everything. Now I just sit lazily and watch eight men fighting eight other men pulling real hard and making awful faces and being yelled at by a little squirt with a megaphone. The finish is spectacular when they all fall in a heap.

But isn't it nice to know that nobody ever got killed rowing?

TENNIS

Tennis is the one sport which should get a cup for improvement in the last fifty years. Coming up from a tiddly-winks and dabs, grassy, pingy-pongy business in bloomers and ice cream pants, it has emerged to a whirlwind finish gymkhana which seems to be only in the province of Australian kangaroos.

Tennis players will tell you that it is the sport of true gentlemen, and a gentlemanly game in which all participants are true sportsmen with nary a quarrel or a quibble or ever such low moments as a brouhaha or a rhubarb.

It sounds good through a mustache but if you ever saw a tennis match you can hardly find the players for the referees, linesmen, judges perched on high chairs, scorers, and various other spies to be certain that the ball is hit fair and proper and received in bounds.

I always thought tennis was sissy and having done a couple of hundred forty, love, deuce games in my time, I still think it's the last of the feudal systems. For example, a handsome dan in tight white pants and a skivvy hits a ball. Immediately the scorers decide what it is, and a couple of juveniles run across the court and retrieve the pellet so that Hermes doesn't have to stoop or break the pose. What other sport has a bunch of handmaidens to do the dirty work? Imagine!

Also, tennis is a ladies' game and don't hit me with a racquet before I explain. Where would the thing be without Eleonora Sears, Molla Bjurstedt Mallory, Helen Wills, Helen Jacobs, Suzanne Lenglen, fancy pants Gussy Moran, Althea Gibson, Maria Bueno, Darlene Hard? Who wants pictures of Tilden, Clothier, Williams, Borotra?

There is something else I wish to say and that is that old tennis players never die, and thank goodness, like Edith Stern. She is still out there, smiling and beating the lace drawers off a lot of teen-age upstarts just like Molla Bjurstedt beat her in 1908 on the Germantown Championship courts 6-1, 6-1 . . .

SUNDAY PAINTERS

Now, by actual computer count of sales of brushes, paints and canvas, there are four hundred thousand, eight hundred and ninety five Sunday painters. Each one has a teacher. Hence the Renaissance. Sunday painters are Big Business and get a lot of bifocals out into the fresh air and they produce a pile of unburnable masterpieces at least so high.

All you have to do to be a Sunday painter is to get a Christmas gift of one of those numbered canvases with "The Mona Lisa" sketched on it, and fill it in, all Winter. By Spring, you are accomplished and comes Summer, you are not only a Master but can talk as wild as a real Modern Artist.

Then, instead of spending money on something useful, like a fine Courvoisier, or a box of Corona-Coronas or a fresh wig, you can invest in Artist Materials. Even the teensiest miniature painter dies leaving a large studio and an accumulation of hard-to-salvage, just-started tubes of expensive oil colors; racks of unfinished canvas, picture frames which don't take stock-size stretchers, enough brushes to dust the Louvre, easels, stools, rolls of fine Belgian linen, and boxes of pencil stubs.

So, having painted nudes indoors all Winter, now it's warm and paintsy outdoors. You pack too much gear and out you go, over hill and dale, through field and forest, across bull corrals and chicken yards. You zigzag cow pastures and watch your step in goat areas, climb rickety fences and survey barns, hayricks, jigsaw houses and curleycue porches, seeking, ever seeking, the elusive perfect composition. Nothing seems just right. You sit and peer and munch your lunch. The sun goes behind a cloud and everything perfect and shadowy is now a dull blank.

Well, you set up your easel, anyway, and spread beautiful lines of color on your palette. Now the sun comes out for a brief moment and you mix a lovely swirl of Alizirin crimson and rich vermillion and calm it with permalba white. You determine to lay a few notes in and finish it at home. A lone pigeon circles and circles your canvas hopefully. Just as you place your maulstick and get ready to take a swing at the canvas the first rain hits you full face.

You pack quickly and slowly drive home. There, right in front of your porch, is exactly the composition for you.

DELAWARE RIVER
BRIDGE

Way back in 1926 A.D. when the world was two lanes wide we had the Sesquicentennial, and the Delaware River Bridge (I know it's now the Benjamin Franklin Bridge) was dedicated by Mayor W. Freeland Kendrick, an old-fashioned Mayor, Elk's tooth and all and none of your goodness and Grand Jury stuff.

The bridge was designed by the great bridge engineers Modjeski, Masters and Chase. Paul Cret, the architect, added the coating and approaches which make it look good.

To appreciate the Beaux Arts idea of the joy of living requires a couple of jereboams of Moet et Chandon champagne, 1878, a very good year, which you can't even get a split of aujourd'hui. So I guess the easiest way to imagine is to somehow, without getting killed by traffic, go to an island along Fifth Street near Race and stand on the grassy eminence like Napoleon at Elba. There, surrounded by big octagonal brass memorials to everybody, look dead East. VOILA. The Delaware River Bridge.

The ribbons of paving used to be flanked by a pair of gorgeous flag poles, capped by golden winged figures bearing aloft the golden garlands of victory of the flivver over the horse. And flying at full billow were the biggest and most beautiful American and Pennsylvania State flags. Gone, the flagpoles are gone to storage and what a pity and what a waste, bring back the flagpoles to me. And beyond you can look to the majestic sweep of the cables over the great steel towers and down to disappear into the stone towers at the ends.

If you can steal a side glance at these stone piers, they are decorated with the armorial bearings of the two states. And within the massive piers, you have to take my word for it, is a fine frieze of decorative tile by Joe Allen, depicting the history of transportation all the way to the Graf Zeppelin.

Of course, when you are heading out of the heat you don't want to stop and look, and when you're coming back to town it's too much to ask of you, but I guess you should know it's there, just in case you want to show the cousins from Oklahoma, which is about the only time I ever look at anything around here myself.

So get your quarter ready for the toll gate, put your head down, stay in your lane, go, go, go. Nine million four hundred and eight pine trees, hot dog and fruit stands, and there ahead are the meadows and salt water taffy and cool air.

KIOSKS

One of the larger "patsies" of the new goody City Charter is the relegation of the authority of the Art Jury to little more than keeping signs and canopies within artistic bounds. Big Deals in the apartment field and others seem to be off-limits to mature Art Jury judgment, and the net result is the city is loaded with pedestrian architecture.

The answer is to give the Art Jury wider powers and back them up. But changes to the charter are idle dreams; so the most that we can hope for is better sign regulating.

It seems crude of me to offer free-of-payola advice to such capable characters as the Art Jury who are so honest that they probably wouldn't take a returned dime from a telephone slot.

But when it comes to "visuals" and designing signs for the betterment of Hoi Polloi I should like to present an old scheme which they use in Paris and so it must be cultural. It is Kiosks.

Kiosks will solve a lot of headaches. They can be useful as well as beautiful and make newspaper and magazine salesmanship a joy to behold, and the circular area is valuable for displays which can be changed at a moment's notice.

For those who have never been to Paris and think that a kiosk has only unmentionable uses, I may say that it is an invention of the Turks and is primarily a newsstand or for the sale of flowers. Where you see them in Paris, Madrid, Lisbon or Baghdad, they are always capped with an "onion" dome.

I know that as soon as I suggest this, the idea is as good as lost because it is probably impractical, expensive, old hat and outmoded. But it certainly would gay up the town. Maybe is better I should go through channels and sell it to *The Bulletin,* instead.

MUSICAL FUND HALL

MUSICAL FUND HALL

Almost as soon as the country got clear of outside entanglements the powdered-wig set organized to encourage music, and of course diffuse taste, whatever that is, and also take care of the families of needy professional musicians already.

And they, in 1824, purchased an unfinished church on Locust above Eighth, and engaged the great architect William Strickland to re-design it. The concert room on the second floor is supposed to have as fine acoustics as the Academy of Music and in a smaller auditorium if anybody cares to argue the point. Ole Bull played there and Jenny Lind sang and also Adelina Patti.

Hardly a man is now alive who can remember when anybody sang there (last concert 1857) but the place is still there, now slightly altered to meet the more pressing needs of a tobacco warehouse.

Of course, this being the age of the big wave toward Kulture, it might be a nice idea if the Society Hillbillies would gang up on the Planning Commission and try to restore Musical Fund Hall. That would take the heat off the City Fathers who are being badgered into the scheme of Super Music Markets, modern glass structures with everything under one roof—air-conditioning, movable acoustic panels, soundproofing fine enough to catch a pin droplet and every breathing moment set for the finest in Modern Moosic.

So what is coming out? Brahms, Bach and Beethoven, all about as "today" as lace drawers and silver buckles.

I guess this thought will kill the idea quicker than you can say Ikelevy, but it was worth a plunk on my harp of a single string.

161

THE ROW HOUSE

I was born in, lived in but probably will not be buried from the front parlor of a row house. I can speak with some sentiment for what was and still is the backbone of Philadelphia city living. There are so many examples of row house architecture that even archaeologists can't make up their minds which is best.

The rise and fall and rejuvenation of neighborhoods is something which gives cushy jobs to City Planners, who mark the maps with pins, showing areas for redevelopment and bettering; and get rocks at their heads for their learned efforts.

But row house living isn't so difficult to comprehend. It is for people who like living in the city at street level. That might mean anything from Grandmom or a midwife delivering the babies, to having no keys to the front door, because otherwise how could Pop roll in at 3 A.M. without waking up the whole neighborhood. And likewise it means a front stoop washed and scrubbed for sitting on so you can easily see what is going on up and down the street, and a "busybody" out the second floor window in case you are making the beds.

The tonier row house set has front porches with wicker furniture where you can garret and gossip, and maybe a city-owned tree at the curb. There is also a backyard society which hangs out wash, raises bargain packets of roses, and casts angry glances at the neighbor's destructive pet cats. And the abandoned outhouse is now hidden by oversize sunflowers.

Just in case somebody wishes to question my authority on row house living, I visited the scenes of my childhood, 8th and Lehigh; Jefferson and Franklin, 8th and Columbia; Grandmom's house at 11th and Poplar; then uptown with trees around, first 17th and then 18th and Erie and swish Abbotsford Road. Then back to 17th and Spruce and down to Camac between Spruce and Pine.

Having gone back to where I came from, now I am a country gentleman—which means you never learn much about the country and soon cease being a gentleman.

And so, like almost everybody else who writes about living in the city I come in, sniff, complain and then ride back to birds, trees and flowers for company.

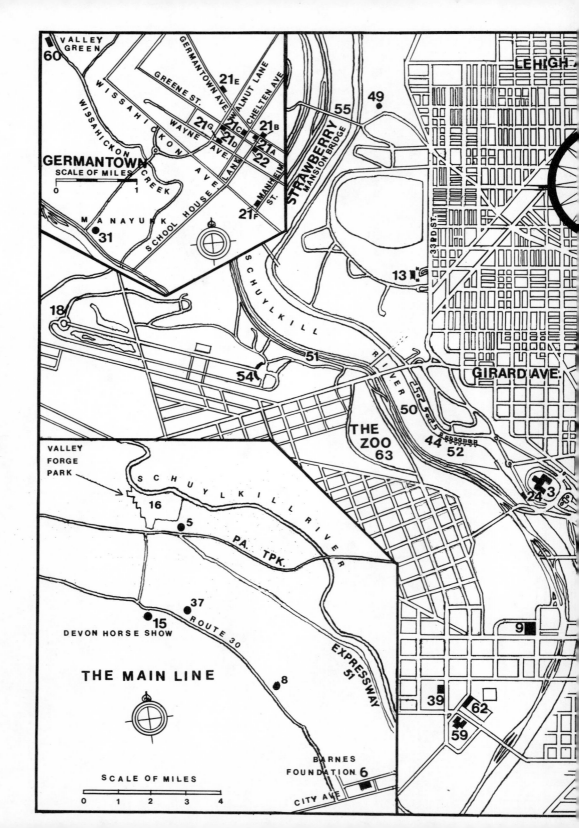

VALLEY
GREEN
60

GERMANTOWN AVE.
GREENE ST.
WALNUT LANE
CHELTEN AVE.
21E

21C 21B
21G 21D 21A
22

WISSAHICKON AVE.
WAYNE AVE.
WISSAHICKON CREEK
SCHOOL HOUSE LANE
MANHEIM ST.

GERMANTOWN
SCALE OF MILES
0   1

55
49

STRAWBERRY
MANSION BRIDGE

21F

MANAYUNK
31

LEHIGH A

33RD ST.

13

18

SCHUYLKILL

RIVER

54
51

GIRARD AVE.

24 3

VALLEY
FORGE
PARK

SCHUYLKILL RIVER

16

5

P A.   T P K.

THE
ZOO
63

50

44 52

37

15
DEVON HORSE SHOW

ROUTE 30

THE MAIN LINE

8

EXPRESSWAY
51

9

39

62

59

BARNES
FOUNDATION   6

CITY AVE.

SCALE OF MILES
0   1   2   3   4